THE GUINNESS GUIDE TO
STEEPLECHASING

THE GUINNESS GUIDE TO
STEEPLECHASING

Gerry Cranham
Richard Pitman
and John Oaksey

GUINNESS SUPERLATIVES LIMITED
2 CECIL COURT, LONDON ROAD, ENFIELD, MIDDLESEX

Editor: Anne Smith

The Publishers would like to thank W. N. Sharpe Limited
who kindly supplied us with a negative for the illustration
appearing on pages 12–13.

ISBN 0 900424 74 5

Published by
Guinness Superlatives Limited,
2 Cecil Court, London Road,
Enfield, Middlesex

Printed and bound in Great Britain by Bemrose and Sons Limited, Derby

Contents

Preface

Gerry Cranham's deep involvement in all aspects of steeplechasing over the last 14 years has produced many rare and exciting photographs. A collection of these has now been brought together to provide a colourful and dramatic insight into this spectacular sport.

The individuals involved in the world of steeplechasing have come to know and respect this photographer who has an almost uncanny knack of being in the correct place at the right time. It becomes increasingly obvious, as the book progresses, that his photographs are always taken in a good setting. This is the result of much preliminary research, planning and careful thought before any action occurs. The many thousands of photographs that have had to be discarded when selecting the illustrations for this book show how many hours he has spent in front, behind, at the side of, above, and *under* steeplechase fences, mostly in cold or damp conditions.

As happens to every rider I underwent a period when I could do nothing right. If I asked my horse to stand off at a fence he would crash through it on the way down, or if I asked my steed to put in a short stride, invariably he would put in one too many and would crash into the obstacle on the way up. Either way the result was the same – I ended up rolling in the grass, and without fail I would see the same grinning photographer every time I rose to my feet no matter which part of the course I was on. Gerry could always be relied upon to give an accurate description of the events leading up to the fall, and then a few days later supply a photographic record of the incident! It was through this series of falls that I came to know Gerry personally, and happily the relationship has flourished over the years to become a strong friendship.

Although heavily committed, John Oaksey graciously agreed to write the first two chapters of this guide to steeplechasing, and both Gerry and I are very grateful to him for setting the scene. The remainder is strictly my own interpretation of racing as experienced and observed over a period of 22 years, ever since the days when race meetings at Cheltenham were the sole reason for my absence from Tewkesbury Grammar School.

In the following pages Gerry and I have tried to produce a general picture of steeplechasing as we have seen it. We sincerely hope you get as much pleasure from reading it as we have had in compiling it over the years – experiencing the triumphs and disasters which steeplechasing holds for all those who choose to follow it, either as participants or as spectators.

Richard Pitman

1 The history and origins of the sport

Ever since men first set out to travel fast across country on horseback they have had to persuade their horses to jump whatever obstacles may be in the way. War and self-preservation were no doubt the first incentives, but hunting — for food if not for sport — is at least as old as time. And it is in hunting — the kind that Mr Jorrocks called 'the image of war without its guilt and only five and twenty per cent of its danger' — that the art of cross-country riding has its roots.

Mr Jorrocks himself, who reckoned a fall 'a hawful thing' and was 'not afraid of pace so long as there is no leaping', cannot really be counted among the pioneers. Even his inventor Robert Surtees, though not as hostile as some other sporting scribes of the 19th century, describes steeplechases (in Mr Sponge's Sporting Tour) as 'generally crude, ill arranged things . . . in which there is always something wanting or forgotten'. But Surtees still made 'The Grand Aristocratic Steeplechase' the climax of Mr Sponge's eventful tour. The hero may have been a somewhat reluctant winner in the end and the man who set out the course was convicted of manslaughter shortly afterwards. But no one who reads a description of that day can doubt that such occasions provided a pretty colourful and exciting entertainment.

The first recorded steeplechase (they got the name because steeples were suitably visible landmarks) was run in County Limerick, a match between two Irish hunting men called O'Calloghan and Blake. They rode from Buttevant church to Saint Mary's Doneraile, the tower of which was known as St Leger steeple. The year was 1752, the distance, like that of a modern Grand National, was 4½ miles. Buttevant church is only a few miles from the farm on which 200 years later Vincent O'Brien began a career which won three consecutive Grand Nationals and has since made him one of the most successful race-horse trainers.

Messrs Blake and O'Calloghan were sportsmen intent on proving their own and their horse's mettle. But that sort of rivalry is as old as hunting itself and from the 17th century onwards, English and Irish horsemen had been challenging each other to 'pounding matches' or 'wild goose chases' — in which, as the name suggests, one rider took his own line as far and as fast as he was able with the other doing his best

to catch him. 'Hard pounding' was how the Duke of Wellington described a crucial stage of Waterloo and even in those days the sporting variety was considered cruel by many — 'For if two good horses are met, the match cannot be tried till one of them is half-spoiled, if not both.'

As hunting changed so did the sport it had inspired, and when foxes replaced stags as the most popular quarry their speed and cunning demanded faster hounds as well as horses. In the second half of the 18th century an infusion of greyhound blood produced lighter speedier packs and, to stay with them hunting men began to use thoroughbred sires on their mares or, in many cases, used pure thoroughbreds as hunters. By this time new agricultural methods had criss-crossed the English countryside with hedges, ditches, stone walls and posts and rails. Jumping was therefore still as important as speed and as the 19th century approached, cross-country matches and challenges became both more common and more hazardous. In 1790 the first actual 'race' as opposed to a 'match' was recorded in Leicestershire — 'eight miles from Barkby Holt to Billesdon Coplow, £100 a side, no rules as to gates or roads, each to come as he could'.

In some of these headlong scrambles a few couple of hounds were laid on to follow a drag, in others a huntsman or whip who knew the country was used as 'Pilot' — sent off with a start and sometimes ordered to wave his handkerchief to show where the fences could best be jumped.

But such precautions were rare and when Thomas Coleman, one of steeplechasing's earliest impresarios, devised the St Albans' chase in 1830 he took care to conceal the flag holders marking the 4-mile course until the start so that no one could spy out the best line in advance. Coleman owned the Turf Hotel at which the St Albans' chase both started and finished and many of the early organised steeplechases owed their existence to local landlords and tradesmen with an eye on the main chance of profit such sporting gatherings might bring.

It was, for instance, a Mr Lynn, landlord of the Waterloo Hotel in Liverpool, who laid out the course at Aintree over which the first Grand National (then called the Grand Liverpool) was run. By 1839, in fact,

Mr Lynn had lost most of his money and his health so the race won by *Lottery* was organised by a committee of notables including Lord Sefton who owned the land and Lord George Bentinck.

Public interest in the new sport was growing fast by now and according to a local observer the roads leading to Aintree 'were crowded as early as nine o'clock. Not a vehicle of any description that could by any means be made to go was left in town.'

But despite the success of that race — during which Captain Becher immortalised both himself and Becher's Brook by falling into it (twice) on *Conrad* — there was no shortage of opposition to steeplechasing in general, and the Grand National in particular.

'It was, no doubt, a very exciting spectacle', the *Liverpool Mercury* said next day, 'but we can no more be reconciled to it on that account than we are to cock-fighting, bull-baiting or any other popular pastime which is attended with the infliction of wanton torture to any living being.'

'A heartless and unsportsmanlike barbarity' was another somewhat overheated description, and even Nimrod the outstanding sporting journalist of the day asked, 'Is it possible that this barbarous pursuit can long continue to be a reproach to the character of Great Britain and Ireland?'

Well it was possible, and although no doubt many aspects of 19th-century steeplechasing — the severity of the obstacles, the marathon distance over which some races were run, and the prevalent use of whip and spur — would certainly be repugnant nowadays, the fact was that both the new sport and some of its leading characters, human and equine alike, appealed very strongly to large sections of the public.

Nor was that appeal confined to the betting fraternity. In 1840 when *Lottery* was running at Dunchurch the great Dr Arnold allowed the boys of Rugby special leave to watch him — and the boys themselves were so enthusiastic that they collected £15 between them to sponsor a local race. *Lottery*, incidentally, used to jump a fully laid dining-room table for the amusement of his owner's guests, and Captain Becher who also seems to have been an entertainer as well as a first-rate jockey and all-round athlete could imitate the voices of almost every known species of animal!

The fame of men like Captain Becher, Jem Mason who rode *Lottery* and 'Black' Tom Oliver did much to make the sport popular. Unlike Mason, a fastidious dandy who always rode in clean white gloves and had his boots made by two different cobblers, one for the legs and one for the feet, Oliver was rough in looks as well as upbringing. 'Off the pigskin, I'm the biggest fool in England,' he once told a magistrate — but his friends knew differently and steeplechasing's greatest poet Adam Lindsay Gordon was one of many who loved as well as admired him:

He cares not for the troubles of Fortune's fickle tide
Who like Bendigo can battle and like Oliver can ride.

Nor do some of Black Tom's recorded sayings sound like those of 'the biggest fool in England.'

'Your horse *can* stay four miles,' he told the anxious owner of some useless animal for instance — 'but he takes the hell of a long time about it.'

Oliver who was Jem Mason's great friend as well as his greatest rival — 'I would fight for Jem up to my knees in blood,' he once said — won three Grand Nationals himself and George Stevens, his pupil and protégé, won five. But although Stevens' achievement made them memorable, steeplechasing went through a period of difficulty and decline in the middle years of the 18th century. Too many small, badly organised meetings sprang up all over the place; the far stricter control of flat racing imposed by Lord George Bentinck and Admiral Rous drove the sharper element to seek easier pickings elsewhere, and if the obstacles had often been too large and dangerous before, now they went to the other extreme until, even at Aintree, as one critic wrote, 'It almost requires a microscope to discover the fences.'

Quite justifiably, opposition to the sport became more vocal than ever. 'No fair bet can be made on a steeplechase,' said the *Sporting Review*, 'It is a mode of racing which we do not recommend.'

The sport's major weakness, of course, was that no generally recognised and accepted set of rules had ever been drawn up and those few which did exist were seldom observed let alone enforced by a strong central authority. The Jockey Club did not even recognise steeplechasing, so whatever crimes a jumping jockey or trainer might have committed he was still allowed free access to the flat racing world.

For a sport which, at that time, depended heavily on serving soldiers the Crimean war was an added disaster. Indeed meetings held in the Crimea itself were far more successful and better organised than those at home.

Happily, however, steeplechasing still enjoyed the loyalty of some honest, intelligent and determined men. Without their efforts in the second half of the 18th century it might, as a correspondent later wrote in *Bell's Life*, the *Sporting Life* of the day, have become 'Synonymous with robbers, with no recognised laws to protect it . . . an instrument of fraud and bare faced trickery.'

The first step towards salvation from that fate was taken by Mr Fothergill 'Fogo' Rowlands a Monmouthshire owner and gentleman rider who initially had horses with Tom Oliver and then began to train them himself. Having tried unsuccessfully to stage a new steeplechase for farmers and hunting men at Market

Harborough in 1859, he succeeded brilliantly the following year. This time twelve different hunts subscribed to the cost of a Grand National Hunt Steeplechase — '£10 each with £500 added; for horses which have never won before starting, 12 stone each, 4 miles'. So the National Hunt Chase was born, and with very nearly the same conditions it is still run today at Cheltenham each March.

Thanks to Rowlands the new race was strictly controlled and efficiently conducted according to rules which he himself drew up and which became known later as 'The Harborough Act'. A fine hotly contested 4-mile race between good horses and keen amateur jockeys over big fair fences was the exact opposite of the dismal depths to which so many so-called steeplechase meetings had sunk. Not surprisingly the public welcomed it unreservedly, and to others with the good of the sport at heart it gave badly needed encouragement.

In November 1862 two of jumping's most energetic supporters, B. J. 'Cherry' Angell and W. G. Craven, wrote to *Bell's Life* suggesting a standard set of rules. The great Admiral Rous, by far and away the most famous and widely respected racing figure of the day, wrote back welcoming the rules in general and suggesting a few alterations.

The Admiral's word was law in those days and, no doubt encouraged by this Olympian recognition, Angell and Craven formed themselves with Lord Grey de Wilton into the Grand National Hunt Steeplechase Committee. History does not relate why they failed to invite Mr Rowlands to join them, but the title of the new committee was taken from his race and his example and sporting philosophy undoubtedly contributed to its foundation.

Even then the first years of the newborn National Hunt Committee (a shortened title which it finally assumed in 1889) were far from easy and its chance of survival, let alone real power, seemed at times remote in the extreme. Both the first two serious disputes referred to the Committee were in the end decided by Admiral Rous, but in 1866 they boldly passed a resolution that 'The decision of the Stewards or whomsoever they appoint is final in everything connected with steeplechases.' They added, 'There is no appeal whatever to a court of law' — although, as Admiral Rous had earlier quite rightly pointed out, 'This is an imaginary edict which would be laughed at even if it came from the Crown.'

Many of the new Committee's edicts were undoubtedly laughed at or, worse still, ignored altogether — but its members soldiered bravely on and gradually in the 1870s began to extend their authority. Many of them already belonged to the Jockey Club and although the attitude to steeplechasing of most flat racing purists was still one of tolerant condescension the Jockey Club did at least recognise that the National Hunt Committee had a right to control its branch of the sport.

That control was much strengthened, at least in theory, by a resolution in July 1875 to pass the following rule:

> Every meeting must be advertised in The Racing Calendar. The advertisement must state that the meeting is to be subject to the Grand National rules and must state as soon as practicable the days on which the meeting is to begin and end and the names of two or more persons as Stewards and of the Judge, Starter, Handicapper and Clerk of the Scales.

But although this meant that according to the letter of the law no meeting could be held without the Committee's permission it did not, in practice, prevent another rash of new ones breaking out in the last quarter of the century, many of them organised or disorganised on the most casual and haphazard lines.

At Totnes you had to swim the river Dart twice in each steeplechase, at Bungay the runners once found themselves galloping through a farmyard full of pigs, and at Wye although a long list of Stewards had been published not one of them turned up. Even at Cheltenham the National Hunt Committee decided that it could not fairly disqualify a man 'For taking the wrong course' since there had been no flags to mark the right one.

Obviously such abnormalities and aberrations could only be removed or at least reduced by the introduction of a more or less standard pattern for all steeplechase fences and courses. But on that subject the steeplechasing world was divided by a violently differing view of attitude and philosophy which in varying degrees has survived to the present day.

On one side the old-fashioned 'sporting' view was that the obstacles in a steeplechase should reproduce as nearly as possible the natural unpredictable hazards of the hunting field. Adherents to this view wanted a thorough test of horse and rider, designed among other things as Arthur Coventry wrote 'to eliminate cast-offs from the flat who would be better employed between the shafts of a cab.' The last thing in the world these sportsmen wanted was a course over which 'cast-offs' could flick with ease at a speed which their beloved but more cumbersome hunters could scarcely hope to match.

The opposite school of thought had come to recognise, however reluctantly, that steeplechasing was now a spectator sport which could only survive by providing a watchable event, the hazards of which were not great enough to discourage spectators from betting. Arguments on these lines have been going on ever since and much the same views are now put forward on behalf of modern 'artificial' point-to-points and 'natural' cross-country races.

But in the 19th century the most urgent requirement

'The Scarborough Steeplechase' by J. F. Herring

was for some control, and in fact at that moment many of the new courses, far from being too difficult, 'natural' or dangerous had so trimmed and manicured their obstacles that they provided neither a test nor a spectacle.

So there probably was not much opposition in 1882 when a special sub-committee recommended minimum standards for fences, not all that different from those which are still in force today.

In every steeplechase of two miles they required at least twelve fences with at least six more in each succeeding mile. Every steeplechase also had to include a water jump, 12 ft wide and 2 ft deep, and in each mile there had to be one open ditch — a fence with a ditch 6 ft wide on the take-off side. At that time these open ditches had no guard rail and the water jump was also often open with not even a small fence or rail in

front. However, by 1902 both these safety measures were introduced and for the first time an official 'Inspector of Courses' had by then been appointed to enforce them.

The man chosen was Thomas Pickernell who had ridden in seventeen Grand Nationals and won the race three times. Like other jockeys, before and since, he apparently used to take the occasional nip of alcoholic 'jumping powder' towards the end of his career, and in 1875 is said to have arrived at the start of the Grand National on a horse called *Pathfinder* with very little idea of which way he was meant to go. But the horse turned out to be well named, Pickernell was no doubt quickly sobered up by the Aintree fences and they won in style.

Whatever the truth of that libellous tale the first Inspector of Courses certainly knew his job and his appointment helped steeplechasing to enter the 20th century looking a good deal less irregular and uncontrolled than ever before.

On the disciplinary front, however, the situation was far less satisfactory. For although several jockeys and trainers were punished by the National Hunt Committee for malpractice around the turn of the century, they were almost invariably men of little account in the social and sporting world. There was a general suspicion — not for the first time or the last — that racing had one law for the rich, and undoubtedly certain more eminent owners, trainers and riders seemed to have been allowed to get away with more than most.

Sixty years earlier, Lord George Bentinck had decided to improve a similar state of affairs in flat racing, and now for jumping too the hour produced the man. Captain (later Brigadier General) Stanley may not have had quite Bentinck's brain or personality but he was certainly not short of courage and, unlike Lord George, he was never accused of stretching or breaking the rules he was so keen to enforce upon others.

During the years Captain Stanley was senior steward of the National Hunt Committee, from 1910 to 1913 the rules *were* enforced without fear or favour on rich, poor, great and humble alike. Men like Tom Coulthwaite who trained three Grand National winners, Percy Woodland who rode two, and George Gunter the leading amateur rider of 1909 all came before the Stewards for breaches of the rules and Coulthwaite, one of the most successful jumping trainers of the era, was actually warned off from 1913 to 1930.

Despite the efforts of Brigadier Stanley and those who came after him it would of course be a grave exaggeration to suggest that National Hunt racing in the 1920s — or indeed at any time before the Second World War — bore much resemblance to the highly organised, heavily subsidised and strictly controlled sport which it is today. The flat race enthusiasts who sneered at jumping as a mongrel designed for 'The needy and greedy' were by no means altogether justified, although in terms of prize money alone

Golden Miller **exercising in the paddock at Aintree in 1935**

jumping certainly was — and still is — very much a poor relation of the flat.

Although many of those who followed and supported steeplechasing were genuine horse lovers racing for the pleasure and thrill of watching good chasers jump at speed, there was also undoubtedly a fair-sized section of more or less professional gamblers in whose methods of earning a livelihood neither the National Hunt rules nor the ten commandments played any noticeable part. For such people the smaller less publicised jumping meetings were both a perfect opportunity and an irresistible temptation. Roger Mortimer in his entertaining and erudite account of the period tells of a trainer who on arriving home from such a meeting sat back with a large drink and told his wife 'I had my ideal race today. There were four runners, two of them I knew weren't trying, one was my own and the other one I had backed.'

At most meetings even with the pound as healthy as it used to be the prize money was ridiculously low. In the 1929/30 season for instance there were, apart from the Grand National, only five races worth as much as a £1000 to the winner, and at many of the lesser country meetings a prize of £100 was exceptional. On the other hand, even quite eminent trainers charged as little as £4 a week to train a jumper. Not surprisingly in these circumstances National Hunt racing had precious little attraction for the sort of rich owners and owner breeders who dominated British flat racing between the wars. But in the 1920s and 30s nevertheless, a handful of rich men and women did begin to take up the sport — including several American sportsmen like

Mr F. Ambrose Clark, Mr J. H. 'Jock' Whitney and Paul Mellon. They found jumping in England very much more entertaining than its even less-developed counterpart in America and they were joined by that remarkable lady Miss Dorothy Paget, while men like Mr J. V. Rank and Lord Bicester were constantly on the lookout for big strong horses of the type likely to succeed at Aintree.

There was then no more shortage than there has been since, or is today, of men keen to ride over fences, whether for a living or for fun. The inter-war period produced great professionals like Dick Rees, Billy Stott, Billy Speck, the brothers Anthony and Gerry Wilson and, over hurdles, George Duller. Several amateurs were very nearly, if not quite, their equal and among these Harry Brown was certainly outstanding. In 1919 he became the last amateur ever to head the list as champion National Hunt Jockey and, like Captain Becher and Squire Osbaldeston he was an all-round sportsmen. Arriving early for Hereford races one day he backed himself to catch the biggest salmon of the season and ride a winner all within one hour. But alas, having landed a 44 lb salmon, he fell at the last fence when riding ten lengths clear on his great and usually reliable favourite *Dudley*.

As regards structure, priorities, and organisation, jumping did not change all that much in the years between the wars. But the class of horse taking part was steadily improving, races began to be run at a faster pace throughout, and a gradual revolution took place in styles and methods of riding and, to a lesser extent, of training.

Tod Sloan had already arrived from America to teach English flat-race jockeys that his method, based on much shorter stirrup leathers and a forward crouch poised over the horse's shoulders was far more effective than the upright long-legged 'mounted policeman' seat which had until then been universal.

The lesson took some time to sink in to the jumping world — largely no doubt because the old method was, rightly or wrongly, believed to give you a much better chance of staying in the saddle when things went wrong and your horse blundered or pitched over one of the stiffer more varied obstacles of the 19th century.

In the 1890s a leading professional, Arthur Nightingall, had been praised for being 'One of the few who can land over a fence with his back almost touching the horse's hind-quarters' and Dick Marsh who trained *Cloister* to win the Grand National wrote, 'If a man with short leathers is to get safely round Liverpool it will be because he is lucky and flukes are on his side.' I wonder what he would have thought, or said, watching Pat Taaffe winning on *Quare Times*, Willie Robinson on *Team Spirit*, or Andy Turnell finishing third in 1974 on *Charles Dickens* with his knees pulled up above the horse's withers!

But that of course was a long way off in the 1920s and at Aintree a fairly extreme backward seat was still reckoned to be advisable to cope with the big fences and drops up to and after the Second World War. Years before that, however, men like Rees, Stott, Wilson and their contemporaries had begun to develop and perfect what might now be called the conventional Anglo-Irish steeplechasing seat. George Duller rode much shorter of course, and practically never varied his forward crouch throughout a horse's leap, but he was almost entirely a hurdle race jockey and his example was only gradually followed over fences. The way style has developed since the war will be fully illustrated and discussed elsewhere in this book but the sort of 'straphanging' which so many old prints and photographs show had already begun to be regarded, quite rightly, in the 1920s as not only unattractive and unnecessary but also painful, uncomfortable and exhausting for the horse and, worst of all, detrimental to his progress.

Aintree, however, was still the dominant centre-piece of jumping and until well after the Second World War the Grand National remained not only by far the most important and valuable steeplechase of the year, but also the only National Hunt race of any kind which really attracted the general public's interest and deserved, like the Epsom Derby, to be called a truly national event.

For any horse with even the faintest hopes of jumping Aintree — and unfortunately for many who have none — the whole season, indeed the horse's whole career, was planned with the Grand National in view. Before Christmas almost all the jumping meetings away from Aintree were humdrum unimportant stuff and many of the leading chasers either did not run at all or were patently a long way from fully

fit. It was only when the National weights were published in February (the great race had been a handicap since 1843) that public interest began to grow and the newspapers concentrated on prospects for Aintree.

Apart from the special glamour and excitement of the race itself the chief reason for this total pre-eminence of the National was quite simply money. It was far and away the most valuable steeplechase of the season — the one truly worthwhile prize a chaser could hope to win. None of *Golden Miller*'s five Cheltenham Gold Cups, for instance, earned his owner Miss Paget more than £607 while the 1934 Grand National which he won in record time with 12 st 2 lb on his back was worth £7265.

The first Gold Cup had been run at Cheltenham in 1924 and thanks mainly to two great horses, *Easter Hero* and *Golden Miller* who monopolised it between them from 1929 to 1936 it did achieve a position out of all proportion to its value. The Grand National, a handicap run over exceptional fences and distance, could never claim to be a genuine steeplechasing championship. Weight and luck played far too big a part for that, and many good horses, *Easter Hero* himself for instance, were either not suited to Aintree or handicapped out of the National with impossible weights.

Nevertheless, it would have been quite unthinkable in those days for a horse to establish the sort of reputation which *Arkle* earned in the 1960s without even once being entered for a race at Aintree.

Despite his evident and brilliant promise (he had already won two Gold Cups) *Golden Miller* was started in the Grand National as a six-year-old. After making several dreadful mistakes he finally got rid of Ted Leader at the second Canal Turn — and yet, although Leader was firmly of the opinion that the big fences would never suit him, he was back the following year for his historic record-breaking victory. Thereafter, alas, events proved that Leader had been more than half-right and although the great horse ran at Aintree five more times he never won there again and only once even completed the course.

Even so thanks to *Easter Hero* and *Golden Miller* the early 1930s were in a way a golden age for jumping and the fame of these two brought the sport wider publicity than it had ever enjoyed before.

When Hitler put a stop to things in 1939, National Hunt racing was still a top-heavy affair unhealthily dominated by the Grand National and still very much a poor relation of the flat. But in the hundred years since *Lottery* and Jem Mason won at Aintree a firm foundation had been laid.

This is not a history book; its purpose is to give an insight into the very different, far more flourishing sport which since 1945 has grown from those foundations.

15

2 Jumping today

The three most important factors in the transformation which jumping has undergone since the Second World War have been television, the commercial sponsorship of races and the foundation of the Betting Levy Board. The first two are of course interdependent because without the far wider publicity which television brings races would not be of anything like as much value for advertisements to their sponsors.

Colonel Bill Whitbread, President of the Brewery and himself a life-long supporter of jumping (he rode in two Grand Nationals and got round both times, when to do so was a real achievement) was the first man to see how the sport could help his business and vice versa. From the moment his company staged the first Whitbread Gold Cup at Sandown in 1957 jumping has never been the same again. Like the Hennessy Cognac Gold Cup which followed in November of the same year the Whitbread was a long-distance handicap steeplechase designed for the sort of horse likely to run in either the Grand National or the Cheltenham Gold Cup. With the appearance of these two races in the Calendar the position of overwhelming dominance which Aintree had so long enjoyed was at an end.

Since 1957 it has no longer been necessary to train every good-staying steeplechaser exclusively for one of two targets in the month of March. The Hennessy run in November gave one alternative near the start of the season and the Whitbread another near its end. In fact both the first Whitbread in 1957 and the latest in 1977 were won by horses (*Much Obliged* and *Andy Pandy*) who had run and fallen at Aintree. But the old top-heavy philosophy by which for almost all good-staying chasers the whole season used to be regarded as a build-up for the National, now only applies to a few dyed-in-the-wool Aintree specialists like *Red Rum*.

The example set by Whitbread and Hennessy Cognac was almost immediately followed by a whole host of other commercial sponsors producing comparatively valuable targets for horses of every kind from one end of the season to the other. From the end of the flat in November until its beginning in March or April there is now scarcely a single Saturday without at least one good, competitive, sponsored steeplechase or hurdle race.

For this satisfactory state of affairs television can undoubtedly claim a large share of the credit, but there is admittedly another darker side to the coin.

It is impossible to measure exactly the overall effect on racecourse attendances of television. But on an average Saturday afternoon nowadays at the height of the jumping season you can sit at home in front of a warm fire and, if sufficiently expert with the switches (or the happy owner of two television sets), watch as many as ten or eleven races on three different courses. Even if the meteorological experts are right in predicting that the British climate has changed for good it would be absurd to deny that, for many people, this sort of luxurious armchair race-going is infinitely preferable to watching six or seven races on a cold, wet winter's day with all the extra expense of travel, entrance fees and the mammoth prices which racecourse caterers now seem to find themselves compelled to charge. But although there can be no doubt that for these reasons many potential paying customers do stay at home instead of going racing it can also certainly be argued that since 24 January 1948 when the BBC first broadcast pictures of two steeplechases and a hurdle race at Sandown, television's services to jumping have far outweighed any harm it may have done.

For one thing, since those early post-war years when racing in general was enjoying the boom which came with peace, BBC and ITV brought the thrill and spectacle of jumping into literally millions of homes where they had never been known before. Up to 1945, as we have seen, the Grand National had, apart from a few heroic figures like *Golden Miller*, been the only real point of contact between the sport and the general public. Only a handful knew from their own experience how exciting and moving it can be to watch men and horses race at speed over fences and hurdles. Now suddenly to countless people whose equestrian knowledge was probably confined to an occasional childhood ride on seaside donkeys this new spectacle suddenly became an exciting, often even a frightening, reality. Television showed that the danger, speed and violence which most people had until then associated only with newsreel films of the Grand National were, for jumping jockeys and their mounts, an almost daily way of life. Again it is impossible to give even

Peter O'Sullevan the unrivalled commentator

Television records racing today

Lord Oaksey, former Champion Amateur Jockey, in his present role as journalist and ITV commentator

Julian Wilson presenter and head of BBC's racing team

Brough Scott, ITV's sparkling presenter and racing correspondent of the *Sunday Times*

Richard Pitman has changed his crash helmet for a trilby in his new role as a BBC commentator and journalist

Dick Francis, former Royal and Champion Jockey, now a world-wide acclaimed novelist

Jovial Ron Hammond, racing photographer

The concentration of John Sharratt *Raceform*'s senior watcher

Never missing from the racing scene, the talented photographer Ed Byrne

Peter Scott racing correspondent of the *Daily Telegraph* pursues a story with trainer Derek Kent

Former trainer Ivor Herbert, journalist and author

Phil Bull, founder of *Timeform* and great racing expert

Pacemaker's correspondent-in-chief Tim Fitzgeorge Parker

Len Thomas, senior reporter of the *Sporting Life*

Charles Benson, The Scout of the *Daily Express*

The innovation of the camera patrol provides the evidence for stewards enquiries and objections

estimated numbers, but for all the potential racegoers who have admittedly been kept at home by television there certainly must have been and must still be a large number of men, women and children who now go racing because they want to see for themselves, in the flesh so to speak, sights and sounds which they first experienced on the television.

But even this incalculable widening of jumping's public by no means exhausts the arguments on the credit side for television. Since the formation of the Betting Levy Board in 1963 the financial health of all British racing has depended heavily on assistance from the Levy — which in its turn depends on betting turnover. And as any Bookmaker will tell you the effect of television coverage on that turnover is immediate and immense. The stay-at-home punter may not pay to go racing but with a telephone to hand he can and still does contribute to its upkeep. Of course he also contributes, unless he is very lucky, to the dividends of big bookmaking companies but that, rightly or wrongly, happens to be how the British public prefers to lose its money! And this, you'll be glad to hear, is neither the time nor the place for arguments about Tote monopolies, etc!

The Whitbread Gold Cup was of course only the beginning of sponsorship. Its success and that of the

Hennessy did not go unnoticed. Six years later the Schweppes Gold Trophy began its sensation-studded life as by far the most valuable handicap hurdle race of the season and soon there was hardly a weekend throughout the winter without several subsidised races advertising their sponsors' wares on television.

Now, despite the gloomy economic climate, during 1977 sponsors contributed 15·8 per cent of all jumping prizes as compared with 9·2 per cent from the racecourses, 22·4 per cent from the owners themselves and 52·6 per cent from the Levy Board. In the sense that its total prize money is only half that offered on the flat, jumping is still 'the poor relation'. But it would be a whole lot poorer — as well as much less varied and exciting — without the help which television and sponsorship continue to provide.

In yet another way television has helped materially to alter the priorities of the jumping year because whatever effect it may have had on racecourse attendances in general, it has undoubtedly been a disaster for Aintree and the Grand National. The great race, run around a two-mile circuit much of it far removed from the stands, had never been an easy one to watch even with high-powered glasses. Only a small proportion of the vast pre-war crowds saw much of the action at Aintree when the visibility was good — and quite frequently it was nothing of the kind. So the moment the BBC began to develop its present wonderfully detailed coverage the temptation to stay at home and enjoy a close-up view of every single fence became difficult for even devoted enthusiasts to resist.

There is no need here to relate the hectic legal and financial switchback on to which the declining fortunes of Aintree as a racecourse launched the Grand National in the 1950s. At the moment, thanks to the expertise of Ladbrokes and Clerk of the course John Hughes — and to the glory reflected by horses like *Crisp* and his unique conqueror *Red Rum* — the National looks like being re-established as what it had always been — the greatest steeplechase there is and one of the world's most memorable sporting spectacles. But it will never again so dominate the jumping season that the rest becomes either dull rehearsal or stale anti-climax. That old regrettable top-heaviness has been removed for good and jumping is as a result both healthier and better balanced than ever before.

But despite the shift in emphasis away from Aintree and the National the climax of the ten-month jumping season still comes in March — at Cheltenham's National Hunt Meeting and at the newly remodelled and rejuvenated Aintree Meeting, all three days of which are now devoted to steeplechases and hurdle races instead of the old 'mixed' combination with the flat. It is still basically Cheltenham, however, which stages the final 'championship' tests for all the various classes and categories of jumpers. For the staying steeplechaser the Gold Cup remains the peak of achievement and for the two-mile hurdler the Champion Hurdle does likewise. Both incidentally are now sponsored — the Gold Cup by Piper Champagne and the Champion Hurdle by Waterford Glass Company.

The *Daily Express* Triumph Hurdle is also the summit for four-year-old hurdlers most of whom would be introduced to jumping as three-year-olds the previous Autumn. The National Hunt Two Mile Champion Chase is what its name suggests, while the Arkle Challenge Trophy and the Sun Alliance Chase provide, over two and three miles respectively, the championships for 'novice chasers' — that is, horses who had not won a steeplechase before the start of the season. The Sun Alliance Novices Hurdle and Waterford Crystal Supreme Champion Novice Hurdle serve the same purpose for 'novice hurdlers' — one at two and a half miles, the other at two. For hunter chasers the Foxhunters Challenge Cup and the Cathcart Champion Chase are run over four and three miles respectively.

Great pains are now taken by the jumping Pattern Committee to provide (with the help of the Levy Board and of commercial sponsors) a series of races in all these categories designed as stepping stones to the top spaced out throughout the season. Once a race has been granted 'Pattern' status it cannot be removed or altered without the committee's permission and the result, though far from perfect yet, is that for any horse good enough to have a real chance of winning one of the 'championships' his trainer should now be able to plan a programme of gainful occupation and, for the novice, progressive education throughout the ten-month season.

That season now starts in late July or early August and continues — on 44 different racecourses scattered all over the British Isles — until the following June. The courses, on 19 of which flat racing is also staged, are now divided as shown in the table.

THE DIVISION OF RACECOURSES
IN THE BRITISH ISLES

Group 1	Group 2	Group 3	Group 4
Ascot	Chepstow	Catterick	Bangor-on-Dee
Ayr	Fontwell Park	Folkestone	Carlisle
Cheltenham	Lingfield Park	Huntingdon	Cartmel
Doncaster	Newton Abbot	Leicester	Devon and Exeter
Haydock Park	Wetherby	Market Rasen	Fakenham
Kempton Park		Nottingham	Hereford
Liverpool		Plumpton	Hexham
Newbury		Stratford	Kelso
Newcastle		Uttoxeter	Ludlow
Sandown Park		Warwick	Perth
		Wincanton	Sedgefield
		Windsor	Southwell
		Wolverhampton	Taunton
		Worcester	Teesside Park
			Towcester

As far as the Jockey Club and Levy Board are concerned the chief purpose of this classification is to lay down the minimum values which, dependent on its group, each course must offer for various types of race. But for owners, trainers, jockeys, racegoers, punters and horses the figure 44 means that British jumping takes place for ten months every year in an almost infinite variety of different conditions. That variety is described in Chapter 3, but however grand or small the course the programmes framed for it are bound to have several things in common.

On each day's jumping, for instance, there must be at least two steeplechases and, from 15 September until the end of the season, one of these must be of three miles or upwards. All the other (non-steeplechase) races must be over hurdles and no race of either kind is now run in this country over less than two miles. (There used to be some one-and-a-half mile hurdle races — often run, as you can imagine, at a pretty furious pace. Their abolition in the 1950s was not, so far as we know, regretted by anyone who ever took part in them.)

Over fences and hurdles alike all races are either handicaps or condition races. In handicaps, as on the flat, each horse is allotted a weight which, according to the handicapper's calculations, should give him the same chance of winning as his rivals. Nowadays each horse is given a 'rating' stored in Weatherby's computer at Wellingborough and one of the official handicappers is responsible for each group or category of jumper. His job is to adjust and update the ratings in that category day-by-day so that when the entries for any particular race are fed into the computer it can immediately produce a ready-made handicap. Since this system was introduced it has often, quite wrongly, been supposed that handicaps are now 'computerised' — the product of a mechanical brain rather than a human one. This is of course utter nonsense. All the calculations on which the handicap is based are still done by a Jockey Club appointed official. He and his colleagues merely use the computer as an electronic notebook — to store the results of their pondering in a quickly obtainable form.

With larger, stronger, older horses and larger jockeys the weights in jumping handicaps are necessarily much higher than those carried on the flat. In all races except steeplechases of three-and-a-half miles or over, the top weight is 12 st 7 lb and the bottom 10 st. With the help of the computer, however, handicaps can now be framed down as far as 21 lb below the permitted bottom weight of 10 st. Then, when runners are declared at the four-day stage (by 12 noon four days before a race) the official handicapper looks to see if the highest weighted horse who has been declared a runner has less than 11 st 7 lb. If so that horse's weight is automatically raised to 11 st 7 lb and all the other declared runners go up in proportion. The lowest weight which can actually be carried is still 10 st but if, for instance, the highest declared runner had originally been given 10 st 7 lb a horse who was handicapped as low as 9 st in the 'extended' list will then be able, by carrying an extra stone, to meet the top weight on the precise terms which the handicapper originally intended.

The only exception to the 35 lb range from 10 st to 12 st 7 lb is for steeplechases of three and a half miles or more. Here the top weight is fixed at 12 st. The bottom weight used to be 9 st 7 lb but so few jockeys nowadays can do that weight that it has been raised to 10 st. If you see that a horse has in fact carried less than 10 st in a handicap it must mean that his rider who if professional, must be under 25 years of age or, if amateur, holds a category 'B' permit in order to claim an allowance of 4 or 7 lb because he has not ridden more than thirty or fifteen winners respectively. The Grand National is the only handicap in which these riding allowances — which are of course designed to help inexperienced riders get going — cannot be claimed. In condition races they cannot be claimed when the guaranteed prize money is £2000 or more.

In hurdle race and steeplechase handicaps the only other possible alteration to the original weight comes in the form of 'penalties'. These are sometimes incurred when a horse wins another race after the original weights were published — a victory which the handicapper had clearly not been able to take into consideration.

In all other races over fences or hurdles the weight each horse carries is determined by the conditions of the race, by his age and by his previous racing record. In outright 'championship' contests like the Cheltenham Gold Cup and Champion Hurdle for instance all horses are meant in theory to meet on level terms. The only difference in weight can be caused by weight-for-age allowances. For example five-year-olds carry 11 st 5 lb in the Gold Cup while all six-year-olds and upwards have 12 st. In the vast majority of condition races on the other hand a horse's weight is adjusted according to his record. The winner of two

The mandatory offering of the winner after a selling hurdle race at Windsor

races — or of one worth a certain amount of money — might for instance have to carry 7 or 10 lb more than the basic weight. Maidens (horses who have not won a race at all) are sometimes also given a special allowance.

As a glance at the racing page of your morning paper will, I am afraid, demonstrate all too clearly, a big majority of all races in jumping programmes are designed for 'novices'. The rules of racing define the word as follows: 'a novice hurdler' is a horse who has not won a hurdle race at the start of the current season, and a 'novice chaser' is a horse who has not won a steeplechase at the start of the current season. Except for a few 'novice handicaps' all novice events are condition races — with a series of penalties added to the basic weight depending on the number and value of races the horse in question has won since the start of that season. A horse remains technically 'a novice' for the whole of the season in which he first wins — and may, alas, stay a novice very much longer if he fails to do so.

Of all the problems from which British jumping now suffers the glut of 'novice hurdlers' — and the corresponding dearth of experienced steeplechasers — is the most urgent, expensive and hard to solve. On every jumping racecourse 'safety limits' are rigidly enforced under which only a certain number of runners can be allowed to start in a steeplechase or hurdle race. As a result, with mammoth three-figure entries for many novice hurdle races, racecourse executives are often forced to 'divide' one race into two, three or four more or less identical divisions. This not only produces a dull, long, uniform programme calculated to bore the pants off even the keenest racegoer, it is also apt to leave the hurdles course like a ploughed field, and in broken hurdles, to say nothing of extra prize money, it costs the racecourses money they can ill afford. The Levy Board has now understandably refused to provide more money for these 'divided' races and for the first time in 1978 the Jockey Club imposed a sliding scale of surcharges which owners must pay on their entries for these races — depending on the number of times a horse has run unplaced. If he has failed to catch the judge's eye six times the surcharge goes up from £1.50 to £3.00. Each subsequent sequence of failure costs a similar jump until for the supreme optimist who still wants to run his horse after eighteen zeroes the surcharge for each entry is £9.00. It remains to be seen whether even this will discourage some of the super optimists on whom jumping has so long relied. But whatever happens the hard fact remains — as we shall see later — that while flat racing provides an unfailing supply of potential hurdlers there simply are not enough purpose-bred potential steeplechasers coming out of the pipeline. The Jockey Club appointed a committee in 1977 to enquire how the breeding and production of this vital raw material can best be

encouraged. But breeding is such a long slow business that however wise and far reaching the committee's recommendations it will be years before their effects will be seen. In the meanwhile, sadly, British jumping courses will continue to be churned up by squadrons of undistinguished hurdlers while all too many of the steeplechases which ought to be their greatest attraction draw only single-figure fields.

Despite this imbalance the average jumping programme still consists of three steeplechases and three hurdle races — even if one of the latter all too often has to be divided at least once. In fact the rules of racing lay down that a minimum of half of the total guaranteed prize money for any particular day must be given for steeplechases.

Within this and various other guidelines the Clerk of the Course has to devise programmes which will not only satisfy the Jockey Club (and his Board of Directors if he has one) but also attract good enough fields to draw a crowd.

After 1 February each year he has one fresh alternative as a new brand of race — the 'hunter steeplechase' begins to appear in the programme. Confined to amateur riders these often eventful contests are condition races for horses which have been 'regularly and fairly hunted' with a pack of hounds during the previous winter. The master of the pack in question has to sign a certificate to that effect and although some of these documents would probably not guarantee the owner's passage through the pearly gates ('he calls "hunted fairly" a horse that has barely been stripped for a trot within sight of the hounds', wrote Adam Lindsay-Gordon) they do give him the right to run his pride and joy in hunter chases.

In fact quite a lot of successful hunter chasers are also genuinely top-class hunters. *Credit Call* for instance, winner of the Liverpool and Cheltenham Foxhunters, carries both Chris Collins and Joey Newton with real distinction across high Leicestershire — and *Bullock's Horn* who completed the same double has actually had the VWH hounds hunted from his back.

Hunter chases are of course a slightly more 'professional' extension of point-to-points — the totally amateur steeplechase meetings which are arranged all over the country by (and usually for the benefit of) the local hunt. There has, as we have seen, always been a close link between foxhunting and steeplechasing. In fact one grew from the other. The link is maintained by hunter chases and point-to-points even if the latter no longer bear much resemblance to the old 'pounding matches' across natural hunting country. They are still quite often effective nurseries not only for horse but also for trainers and for jockeys.

The arrival of the first hunter chases is traditionally greeted each year with groans of apprehension from punters who understandably find it hard to work out

A spectacular leap by *Red Rum* over Becher's Brook in the 1974 Grand National

Jockey Tommy Kinane displays his trophies donated by
the sponsors, Waterford Glass, after winning the 1978
Champion Hurdle

form shown in some distant point-to-point — and who
in any case dislike risking their money on unknown
and, in their view, unpredictable amateur riders.

But although their worst fears are sometimes
justified, the truth is that, 'hunter' form works out at
least as well as that of 'professional' chasers. A reliable
point-to-point form book is now available and while
not all the jockeys involved look much like Stan
Mellor, Fred Winter or John Francome they include a
good few pretty tough experienced horsemen. The fact
that most of them still claim the full 7 lb allowance —
having not ridden ten winners under rules — does not
by any means necessarily prove incompetence. Point-
to-point winners do not count for allowance-claiming
purposes and although it is usually wise to avoid portly
owner riders putting up several pounds unnecessary
overweight the hunter chase can, if you take a little
trouble and use reasonable common sense, be the best
betting proposition of the day.

Apart from selling races — after which the winner is
put up for auction and in which any other runner can
be 'claimed' and bought for a certain sum — the only

other 'oddities' you are likely to find on a modern
jumping card are amateur races (quite a few are held
throughout the season besides the hunter chases) and
'opportunity races'. Each course is compelled by the
rules to put on at least one of these for every four days'
racing it stages during the season. An 'opportunity'
race is confined to professional jockeys who have
not ridden more than a certain number of winners.
Winning one of them does not count towards losing
your allowance — nor does the winner get a penalty for
any future handicap. The races are, as their name
suggests, designed to give young professionals a
chance to get experience.

That then is the framework on which the ten-month
jumping season is built. In an average season for
weather and cancellations about 2500 races are run on
the 43 British courses. Six thousand, three hundred
and eighty-seven individual horses ran over fences or
hurdles in 1976 (averaging nearly five runs apiece). In
1977, 365 professional trainers held jumping licences
quite apart from 530 'permit holders' who are allowed
only to train horses 'the sole property of themselves,
their spouses, parents, sons or daughters'.

These statistics give an impression of a flourishing
sport and there is certainly no sign that jumping is any

Mrs Fred Rimell receives the Piper Heidsieck Cheltenham Gold Cup following *Royal Frolic*'s victory in 1976

less popular now than it has ever been. The sport and those who make their living from it have, on the other hand, excellent reason to think that they are in many ways unfairly treated. In a submission to the Royal Commission on Gambling the National Trainers Federation made the following points:

1. In terms of entertainment, whatever your view of its superiority as a spectacle, jumping provides as many races as the flat and generates 48 per cent of the total betting turnover.
2. Despite these facts jumping receives 57 per cent less prize money than the flat and is given only 35 per cent of the Levy Board's prize money pool.
3. Professional jumping trainers whose costs now are similar to their flat race colleagues receive 19 per cent less in training fees. They can expect to win 80 per cent less in win bonuses (their percentage of winning prize money) than their flat race counterparts and they face competition from permit holders whose livelihoods are not dependent on racing. Only 25 per cent of all

jumping trainers make any profit on their basic training fees.
4. Although jumping jockeys earn more in basic riding fees than their flat counterparts only 10 per cent of them had gross earnings (in 1975/76) of more than £5000.
5. Although stable lads in jumping yards are subject to the same minimum wage structure their opportunity of win bonuses represents only £165.00 per stable as against £1000 on the flat.
6. Quite apart from the huge differences in prize money (the average value of jumping races is less than half that of those on the flat) jumping owners have little or no opportunity to recover their original capital investment. There is almost no resale value for any jumper however successful.

When you consider all these inequalities — and remember that the National Trainers Federation recommended £45.50 as the basic weekly training fee in 1977 for jumpers as well as flat race horses — it seems more than ever miraculous that so many owners are willing and able to pay that kind of money with so little chance of breaking even — let alone of making a profit. In fact, inflation has roared on forcing the top southern trainers to charge a basic fee of £60 for the 1978/79 season. But so far, touch wood, the miracle keeps happening.

Since the formation of the Levy Board in 1961 the control of all racing has been shared between that body, three of whose members are Government appointed and the self-elected Jockey Club with which the old National Hunt Committee was amalgamated. The senior steward of the Jockey Club and the chairman of the Levy Board are now co-chairmen of a Joint Racing Board made up of the Jockey Club's two deputy senior stewards and the two Levy Board members appointed by the Home Secretary.

It would be a grave exaggeration to say that relations between these two very different governing bodies have always been entirely smooth or amicable. Indeed during Lord Wigg's reign at the Levy Board their disagreements were sometimes both public and acrimonious. But it was thanks to Lord Wigg that the Betting Levy is now calculated on bookmakers' turnover instead of their profits and together, even if they did not always see eye to eye, he and the then senior steward Sir Randle Feilden presided over a period of rapid modernisation and improvement for racing in general and jumping in particular.

The Jockey Club remains responsible for appointing all racing officials such as stipendiary steward's secretaries, judges, handicappers, starters and clerks of the scales. They also license all trainers and jockeys and the discipline of the whole sport is still in their hands. Published in 1978, the Royal Commission on Gambling has suggested quite a few radical changes including the formation of a central governing body made up of a selection from the present controllers plus a few 'new brooms'. They also recommended that the ownership of all racecourses, except Ascot, be held by the ruling body. However, it will take many years to complete their proposed changes — if indeed they are ever inaugurated.

On each day's racing the Jockey Club is represented at the course by three voluntary stewards who are themselves assisted by a professional steward's secretary. It is these local boards which enforce the rules of racing on the racecourse.

In this crucial role they are nowadays enormously assisted by patrol cameras which, at two courses on every racing day, film large parts of each contest from two and sometimes three different positions. In jumping races objections and disqualifications can only be justified (apart from intentional foul riding) by events at or after the last fence or hurdle. Now, where the camera is in operation, the stewards have immediate access to two films of what happened on the run-in — one taken by a head-on camera which shows any deviation from a straight line and the other broadside on to show how far apart the horses were when the deviation or interference occurred.

There is no doubt at all that these patrol films, difficult though they often may be to interpret, have greatly improved the standard of racecourse 'justice'. They also make it both dangerous and difficult for any jockey to do less than his best in the closing stages of a race. No one denies that horses are still occasionally given 'easy' races with the devious object of deceiving either the handicappers or the bookmakers or both but it is fair to claim, we think, that by and large the British punter gets a better, straighter run for his money than ever before.

With the help of Levy Board funds great progress has also been made in the fight against doping. At one time in the fifties and early sixties there were several horrid cases in which well-fancied, well-backed horses were undoubtedly and criminally 'got at' to prevent them winning. Obviously undesirable as it is on the flat this is a really unforgivable crime with a jumper — who, half blinded by the drug he has received, may be completely unable to see the obstacles he is being asked to jump.

Thankfully, so far as we know, no jockey was badly hurt in the cases which came to light and nowadays through greatly improved security both at racecourse stables and training yards 'nobbling' seems to have been stamped out.

So, almost certainly, has 'doping to win'. All winners are officially tested — along with any other horse about whose running or behaviour or appearance the stewards are not satisfied. In 1977 the Jockey Club's analysts achieved a major breakthrough when they evolved the first effective method of post-race testing for anabolic steroids. Four horses were disqualified but no further positive tests have yet appeared and it seems at least reasonable to hope that steroids (which had been undetectable and were being pretty widely used) are now confined to their proper veterinary purposes — and only administered long enough before the horse runs to ensure that no trace of the drug can possibly remain in his system.

Of about 11 000 horses in training in the British Isles more than 6000 continue to run over fences or hurdles each season. No other country in the world has anything like so many jumping horses — or so many jumping races for them to run in. The unique sport of which Messrs Blake and O'Calloghan's cross country joy-rides sowed the seeds 226 years ago is alive and well in England, Scotland and Ireland. In an age of inflation, motor cars and supersonic jets it may sometimes seem to be struggling to keep its place but there is no sign that we can see yet of any permanent or serious decline in the enthusiasm on which that place depends.

Rag Trade in the winner's enclosure after the 1976 Grand
National with his jubilant connections

The field take Becher's Brook on the first lap of the 1968
Grand National

Amateur rider Chris Tregoning weighs out on antique scales before his race

Money changes hands on the favourite, *Sheer Courage*

The Old Berks point-to-point meeting shows the popularity of the sport with very few spaces in the car park

Lady riders were riding 'between the flags' long before their acceptance under rules

3 The stage

The stage is the racecourse. In Britain they vary considerably in size, shape, gradients and state of ground conditions. Courses can be put into groups — serious racing (group one), bread-and-butter racing (group two) and holiday racing (group three). Even then attributes and hazards of each member of the three groups vary tremendously. Each course caters for its participants and customers as best it can, though many find the astronomical cost of rebuilding antiquated grandstands beyond them. However, because steeplechase enthusiasts go primarily for the sport, they put up with many discomforts that would not normally be tolerated anywhere else in the world.

There are three types of fence in an English steeplechase. The regulation fence which is a minimum of 4 ft 6 in high is nicely sloped on the take-off side by means of a gorse belly. Usually there are orange-painted rails, both along the foot of the fence and halfway up it to give a horse a ground line so that he hopefully, with the aid of his jockey, measures the approach to perfection.

The second type of obstacle is an open ditch, which as its name indicates has on the take-off side an open ditch. Although guarded by a rail, again in order to give the horse a good idea where to take off from, many racecourses have now filled the ditches in, leaving the same width to jump with the danger to fallers minimised. Horses seem to jump open ditches better than regulation fences, probably because they are more feared by the jockeys, resulting in extra caution and less chances taken. However, when horses do fall at an open ditch they are generally far worse falls than at a regulation fence.

The third type of fence is the water jump, a 12-foot spread following a small brush fence, which horses meeting on a normal stride should have no problem in clearing.

Most horses, before going steeplechasing, will race over hurdles. These are uniform, 3 ft 6 in high, but they do vary from course to course by the amount of slope that individual groundsmen allow when knocking them in. They are jumped much faster than steeplechase fences and can be knocked down, whereas a steeplechase fence usually remains standing when the offending horse and rider are rolling along the grass.

However, a swinging hurdle, that is to say a hurdle that has been knocked flat by a leading horse but has not actually come out of the ground, can sometimes, especially when the ground is firm, swing back, and if a following horse is in full flight when the hurdle comes back, it whips the horse's feet from under it.

Horses are generally more tightly bunched in hurdle races so that falls, though occurring less often, can be of greater consequence. Hurdling is the kindergarten of steeplechasing, but many of the participants fall by the wayside by the time they are old enough to go steeplechasing due to unsoundness, or purely a 'touch of the slows'. Horses may run over hurdles in the August of their third year, and in steeplechases when they are four years old. A steeplechaser does not reach his prime until he is about eight years old, whereas a hurdler is at his best from five to seven years of age, although this of course can vary with the make and shape of the horse.

Of the three Scottish racecourses, **Perth** is the sportiest, in fact it commands that title throughout Britain. Here the heads of Clans can be seen in all their splendour enjoying a complete view of the course, first-class catering facilities and a friendly atmosphere all in the charming surroundings of Scone Palace, bordered by the River Tay. Almost circular, the course rides fast and winners mainly come from the leading group on the second circuit. Jockeys going well enough at the fourth-last fence can often see salmon leaping in the Tay, whereas those riders not going well are so preoccupied with improving their position they just see the backsides of the leaders, but win, lose, or draw, the sporting racegoers of Perth invariably cheer home the leading horses, even if they have lost their investment. This attitude is in sharp contrast to the punters at **Plumpton**, Sussex, who have on several occasions in recent years caused jockeys on beaten favourites to wish they had found that little extra effort that would have forced their fancies over the finishing line to win, even though the rider may have performed near miracles during the race to keep the partnership intact.

Overleaf:
The electric atmosphere as the contestants parade at the Cheltenham Festival Meeting

The public throng the parade ring during the festival meeting at Cheltenham

Keen racegoers become more involved by watching from the inside of the racecourse

So many regular racegoers watch a race without actually 'reading' the happenings which lead to the eventual result.

The stewards of Perth racecourse are all keen racehorse owners themselves. They have numbered amongst them many successes, and the names of Lord Kilmany, Colonel Dewhurst, the Duke of Atholl, Mr G. B. Sanderson, Wing-Commander Stevenson, the Earl Cadogan and David Whitaker, whose wife Fiona owned the 1978 Grand National winner *Lucius*, are equally well known and respected south of the border. Such is their enthusiasm that in times of dry weather each one has sent the water-carts their farmers use for supplying water to outlying cattle to help water the course to ensure that the public enjoy every one of the limited number of Perth fixtures.

Both of the other two Scottish jumping tracks, Kelso and Ayr, are left-handed tracks, the opposite way around to Perth, catering for horses which favour leading with either fore leg; equally it caters for those which 'hang' left or right.

Ayr on the West coast is situated in a pocket and is caressed by the tail-end of the Gulf Stream, thus ensuring that racing is able to be held there when other courses are unable to race because of snow or frost. The Scottish prestige races are held there, including the Scottish Grand National and the Scottish Champion Hurdle. The course is not unlike Newbury, providing a true guide to a horse's form. The prize money is considerably greater at Ayr than at the other two Scottish jumping courses, and likewise the grand-stands are far more extensive to accommodate the larger crowds, which include a greater percentage of the betting-motivated racegoers. Quite rightly Ayr qualifies as a group one racecourse, namely serious racing, and affords typical Scottish hospitality to the many visitors from England. Of the thirteen courses south of the Scottish border, to the north of Southwell in Nottinghamshire, four, namely Newcastle, Doncaster, Haydock Park and Aintree rate as members of the first group.

Aintree is almost criminally reduced to one race meeting per year due to the uncertainty between owners, would-be owners and liquidators. It has an atmosphere that can only be described as 'electric'. The three-day meeting, climaxed by the Grand National, has grown amazingly in stature since the bookmaking firm Ladbrokes took a seven-year lease to run it. They have found substantial sponsors for the races which has in turn encouraged the jumping stars to participate, which entices the paying public back through the turnstiles. The fact that they are an ever-increasingly successful public company, means that they have a fully competent managerial and pro-motional staff at their disposal. I say that it is almost criminal that there is only one meeting a year because the turf at Aintree is superior to that on any other British racecourse. To a 10-stone human being the difference is immediately apparent when walking over it, so to a half-ton equine it must be proportionately noticeable. There is an in-built spring to the turf as a direct result of good grass husbandry, a large area to race over which is not being over-used, and most important the grass has remained unploughed far longer than any living human being can remember.

The course at Aintree is only used for three races a year, namely the Grand National, the Topham Trophy and the Foxhunter's Steeplechase. The latter two are run two days prior to the Grand National, and over just one circuit of the course. The inevitable result of reduced racing there is that young riders and horses are denied the opportunity of riding over the different turf and fences that they will hopefully encounter one day in 'the world's greatest steeplechase', the winning of which guarantees a rider a world-wide passport in 'horsey' circles. The whole course is designed to catch out the young or over-confident rider and horse, with each year's running just adding fuel to the burning passion that true steeplechase followers harbour. Therefore, the Grand National cannot, no, must not, be allowed to become a thing of the past! The build-up to the race is enormous. To a trainer with a runner in the race, the knowledge that his work over the previous year is then totally in the hands of someone else is unsettling. Some even admit to being relieved when their representative is called as a faller, others silently pray as each major obstacle is reached, while old hands at the winning stakes experience a tingling in their spine should their horse still be in the reckoning when the survivors swing onto the racecourse proper for the last time. For a rider there is nothing equal to this race, partly because of the intricacies of the course itself, partly because the huge field consists largely of many doubtful finishers which provides unpredictable moving hazards, and lastly because some very good jockeys possess not-so-good records around Aintree. For the revitalised paying public the conditions are poor; after a fifteen-minute fight to secure a drink it later takes a further ten minutes to reach a toilet. If you choose to see the contestants in the parade ring it is likely that you will not see the race properly, or should you take your vantage point early enough there is little chance of ever getting back to ground level to see anything but a cloud of steam where previously the winner had stood. However, punters, trainers, jockeys, stable staff and owners (who are not even guaranteed a clear view of the race) find that once bitten by the Aintree 'bug', there is no antidote.

In this northern group the Lancashire racecourse, **Haydock Park**, has a regular supply of top-class races and also possesses its own peculiarities. The hurdle

Overleaf:
The famous uphill finish at Cheltenham

Holiday racing at Cartmel in its unusual setting.
Sponsorship is needed in racing, but it should be used in
moderation

course is totally flat and rides fast, even when the rest of the country is flooded, and is considered by most established riders as being a short two miles. This is in sharp contrast to Carlisle and Hexham which are also in this section of England. Both the latter-named courses have steep descents, and even steeper ascents on which to finish, taxing a doubtful stayer's stamina or helping the occasional tortoise to beat the hare.

Haydock's chase course was once greatly respected and in some cases even feared by the jockeys, but today, although the fences with drops on the landing side still threaten to catch out unwary partnerships, they are generally much softer, being not so tightly packed with birch, which is itself far more leafy than that previously used. *Red Rum*'s uncharacteristic monumental blunder at the twelfth fence in the 1978 Greenall Whitley Chase would have upended him ten years ago. Neither I nor anyone else who has the good of the sport at heart, want to see the horses fall, although I am not sure that soft fences are the answer to that particular problem. Often the horse that finds it can get away with a low jump will try it again sooner or later, with unfortunate results. However, Haydock does produce top-class chases as well as attracting the best hurdlers, and operates regularly throughout the winter months providing an important service to British jump racing.

The inaugural running of The Royal Doulton Handicap Hurdle on May Day 1978, valued at £25 000, attracted the first four from the Champion Hurdle, as well as nineteen others whose connections were willing to take on the stars, in view of the race being a handicap, giving everyone theoretically an equal chance of winning. The quality field tempted so many people to leave their homes in every direction that all roads for miles around the course were blocked. The race against time took panic proportions as scores of trainers and jockeys realised they would not get to the course on time in their cars. With Reg Hollinshead giving a lead by 'Shanks's pony' (walking) for the remaining two miles, the tide swelled to include many racing personalities whose usual exercise is restricted to a shuffle from their own front door to the car seat. The whole day was a complete success, and it is to be hoped that it remains an important part of the National Hunt fixture list being assured of attracting the cream of the hurdlers with a good likelihood of the race being held due to the time of year. Fred Rimell's *Royal Gaye* won in a record time, with that season's champion, *Monksfield* (gave 2 stones) in second place, and the former dual champion, *Night Nurse* battling on in third place. Having won every handicap worth winning, Fred will, I am sure, follow his usual pattern of supplementing his May Day success.

Previous page:
Fontwell Park — August Meeting

Hexham, briefly mentioned earlier, has several characteristics which add to the sport, a sport which is so often a game of chance. Situated to the west of Newcastle, close to Hadrian's Wall, Hexham is typical of the many rural racecourses insomuch as it supplies steeplechasing to the locals who are mainly made up from landowners, farmers and hunting men. They are not likely to break any box office records but their support of the local racecourse, no matter what the weather and with little or no plush amenities to tempt them, keeps the whole thing ticking over. Some of the landowners who support racing there are probably wealthier than many of the 'city gents' who race at the urban racecourses, but they do not go to display the latest fashions, purely to enjoy the racing from the natural hillside grandstand, where they are sure to meet many of their friends. Dressed to combat the weather, which they consider incidental, they represent the hardcore of racing supporters, and will pass on to their children, as they themselves were taught, the importance of keeping country pursuits alive. The course itself is a test of stamina, not only because of its steep gradients but also because more often than not the wind decides to save its strength for racing days.

Jockeys are well known for offering what to them seems a feasible excuse whenever a race does not quite go to plan, even if they do not exactly believe it themselves. However, can you imagine an astonished owner believing his jockey's post-race description of, 'Absolutely running away three fences from home, stood off too far, had to stretch to get there, and just as I thought we were regaining our balance the strong cross-wind blew us over.' It sounds absurd I know, but it has happened at Hexham on several occasions, even though the stewards take every precaution and on occasions even abandon meetings when the wind is considered too strong for safety. The times that this unusual excuse is feasible is when for reasons mentioned in Chapter 8 and 9 a horse is off-balance on landing, without further hindrance it may have recovered, but if in danger of toppling over, the cross-winds seal its fate.

Another feature of the course is the separate spur used for the finish of races, a feature which twice during my career has cost southern jockeys a race. The back straight is entirely a steepish descent which causes those horses on the bridle to 'get the run' on their riders, and similarly those which have felt the pangs of tiredness find their half-ton weight forcing their flagging bodies to increase pace at a time when their minds are sending out slow-down signals. The result is that the whole field negotiates the back straight faster than is planned. sweeping round the last bend, only to be faced with two alternative tracks. At this point, several years ago, a southern jockey who had been solely preoccupied with survival throughout the headlong scramble down the hill, suddenly found

Cartmel — having jumped the last fence the field race around the wood before finishing

himself in front and faced with a choice of course, he turned to his nearest pursuer, Paddy Broderick, and shouted, 'Do we go round again?' to which Broderick replied, 'Yes, it's a long way yet, you want to reserve a bit'. You guessed correctly, the awful moment of truth dawned on the leader when having taken the left-hand fork, he saw the rest of the field hard on the smiling Broderick's heels as he drove for the finish on the correct track. An expensive mistake whichever way you look at it, and an inexcusable one! In a similar position Fred Winter tells his jockeys, 'We can all make mistakes, don't worry too much, but if you make the same mistake twice, start worrying about your next employer!' Sound advice from a man who puts a premium on loyalty, and practises exactly what he preaches.

In the same area as Hexham is **Cartmel** which is best described as a holiday meeting. They race on just four days a year — two two-day fixtures, the spring and summer Bank Holidays. This pleasant venue is unique in several aspects, and is strongly recommended for racing fans wanting a full weekend's enjoyment. Situated at the southern end of the Lake District, Cartmel is in a really picturesque setting. It is a sharp

track just over a mile in circumference, and it has, except for Aintree, the longest run-in in England. Having jumped the last fence the field race away from the grandstand, out into the country, skirting a wood, before turning back on their tracks to the winning post. The racecourse is on the edge of the town hard up against a row of cottages whose occupants enjoy the best view possible of the racing whilst entertaining their friends and relatives to a pot of tea and some local potted shrimps.

To ensure that the stewards have a complete picture of the happenings of each race, their representatives are placed at strategic points around the track on small stands, carrying out the job that the camera patrol does on the larger courses. The Dickinson family originated from the area and are very much the local heroes, supporting Cartmel by having runners at every meeting. As well as Tony Dickinson, Cartmel attracts such trainers as Ginger McCain and Arthur Stephenson, all three sporting the traditional headgear of the north, the flat cap as opposed to the southern trilby. It is usually picnic weather and the holiday crowds stay long after racing has finished, in direct

Overleaf:
Racing against March sunset at Warwick races

43

Contrasting conditions between summer and winter
meetings
Top: Devon and Exeter. *Below*: Sandown Park

contrast to the mass exodus at the majority of racecourses at the moment that the horses in the final race have crossed the finishing line. Due to the nature of the Cartmel crowds, jockeys are prepared to expect anything on the track from a football or a model aeroplane, to a small child who has dodged its mother in an attempt to pick daisies on the course.

Sunday can be spent touring the lakes and mountains which have ample eating facilities en route. Bank Holiday Monday is a full day with a hound trail meeting held adjacent to the racecourse in the morning to put punters in the mood for the afternoon's horse racing. Hound trailing is an extremely popular and thriving sport in the area. Bred especially for trailing, the hounds are similar to foxhounds in looks, and they also possess superb scenting powers which enables them to follow an aniseed trail laid by a runner prior to the off. About twenty hounds are released together, painting a fine picture as they race away in full cry. Handlers, owners or 'grockles' (holiday makers) watch through binoculars as the hounds follow the trail across hillsides, occasionally disappearing from view in woods or gullies. Cries of 'Patch is leading, but he will never hold that pace', or 'Park's black bitch is handy enough to win from there,' fill the air. The bookies who have relieved all present of a great deal of cash before the trail, carry on betting even after the half-way stage in the event, which takes approximately twenty minutes to run. Heavy backers have men placed around the trail to evaluate certain hounds' chances. When the hounds have passed half-way, several cars will sweep into the viewing area, and after hurried mutterings between driver and punter, bets may or may not be placed, according to the information given. It is a lovely sight to anybody, let alone those with hounds taking part, as the leaders swing down the hillside, jumping stone walls or streams at full stretch, on the run to the finish. But as with horse racing it is not always the long-time leader who collects the prize — some hounds are shy finishers. Having raced over the wild open terrain they are faced with a crowd of humans all shouting or whistling, with the handlers shaking small trays of meat to encourage them and making more noise than anybody. There is the usual jubilation from the winner's connections, and excuses from the disappointed owners of the beaten hounds. Tales of bad luck filter through, as the country marshalls arrive back from their positions where they were placed to see that foul play is ruled out. When hounds run out of sight into a wood it has in the dim and distant past not been unknown for people to alter the hounds' positions, by means not found in the rule book. Winning bets are settled immediately after the race, before men and hounds alike relax, and then thoughts are turned to the horse racing in the afternoon — definitely a weekend to be recommended.

Of the remaining twenty-eight jumping courses situated below a line between Bangor-on-Dee in North Wales, to Market Rasen on the East Coast, we have a wide variety of courses catering for all types of horse, and likewise for the racing public. It is noticeable that the grade one courses are all situated on large sites, with the lesser grade tracks often crammed into small areas. Character plays a large part in the success of a course as far as public support goes. For example, **Leicester** racecourse is a decent course but it has no outstanding features. Its grandstand is situated at the end of a straight immediately on a bend, causing the public to have too much head-on racing, which provides no spectacle at all. Leicester racecourse is also unfortunate since it has more than its fair share of Monday fixtures, which in all adds up to a majority of very ordinary racing, except of course for winning punters, owners, trainers, and jockeys, and without exception the Horse Race Betting Levy Board who stand to gain a lot of money whenever racing takes place.

In betting shops all over the country tens of thousands of people bet on races, whether they are run at Leicester on a wet Monday, or Cheltenham on a sunny Wednesday. To a great deal of the 'stay at home' punters who use the betting shops, and thus keeping Levy turning over, horses are horses no matter what course they are running on, so it is vitally important that we keep sufficient racecourses in operation to ensure a healthy number of meetings held daily. With our unpredictable climate, it is necessary to have the present number of courses to keep racing going with the minimum of two race meetings a day. Inevitably jumping races are abandoned across the country throughout the winter for various reasons ranging from frost to water-logged conditions, and later on in the season sun-baked ground. Another reason for retaining the courses we have at present, no matter how humble they are, is that they provide an important service to the locals in the area, helping to bind communities together. The Midlands are particularly well catered for by the racecourses. Within quite close proximity, there are Southwell, Nottingham, Uttoxeter, Wolverhampton, Leicester, Ludlow, Worcester, Hereford, Warwick, Huntingdon, Stratford, Cheltenham, Towcester, and not too far away Chepstow; so all in all the Midlands National Hunt fans are well catered for. A surprising aspect is that there are remarkably few racehorse trainers in the Midlands, and those that are there are pretty well spread out.

Warwick racecourse is a very attractive place, and although having mainly middle-of-the-road racing is probably best known for its long-distance chases which are run regularly throughout the year. It is not the most popular course with jockeys, though to the spectator it always provides plenty of incidents. The stands are centrally placed, and the ground, though

Handpainted Jockeys' Board at Chepstow

once known for being bottomless on the entrance to the back straight has, after much work, improved out of all recognition. Practically all the fences can be seen from the grandstands, which though not lavish, have extremely good catering facilities. This is one aspect of racing that, in the majority of cases, needs immediate attention on a large scale in order to encourage the family man to make return visits.

From the jockey's point of view, the fences down the back straight come very close together and are not particularly wide, giving the impression that they are higher than normal. The race really starts on the entrance to the back straight, and with fences narrower there than anywhere else it is always a worrying time for jockeys, in addition to which there are running rails on the inside but not on the outside of the fences, leaving an escape route for horses who might possess such a frame of mind. The course is almost triangular in shape, and when the runners swing for home to face up to the last three fences interest intensifies since the fences are fairly close together, and in true chasing tradition, all else being equal, he who jumps best wins.

There are many enjoyable days to be had at Warwick racecourse during the jumping season, and it has a very healthy club membership which supports on a regular basis, consisting mainly of the local farmers.

The newly built Grandstand at Sandown Park heralding the changing face of racing

Bookmaker at Grand National

There are usually three enclosures at each racecourse catering for people from all walks of life. The annual club members who pay a seasonal fee enjoy the best facilities which, if used every time a course stages a meeting, works out to be an extremely cheap entertainment. The second enclosure, Tattersalls, which always surrounds the parade ring and houses the rows of bookmakers who make British racing both colourful and exciting, provides a complete service to racegoers, accessible by a daily charge. The large betting combines operate in Tattersalls with their pitches on the railings between that enclosure and Members, betting with credit customers and placing telephoned bets from their betting offices amongst their colleagues to bring down the starting price of horses which involve them in heavy financial commitments. The third and cheapest enclosure is either tacked onto the end of Tattersalls under the name of Silver Ring, or occupies a position on the inside of the racecourse and nicknamed 'The Cabbage Patch'. Here, in return for cheap admission, the public have to rough it in comparison to the other two enclosures. They do have both bookmakers and the Totalisator to bet with, but can not get to the parade ring to evaluate the horse's condition, though this can often be a blessing in disguise.

49

Tic-tac man relays the odds

Bookmaker Charles James operating on a cash basis

'Rails' bookmaker John Banks providing credit facilities for both the members and the public

Not far away is **Worcester** racecourse. It is not unlike Newbury, and I think one day, with the help of television coverage, will attract more sponsors than it has at present, although the hard-working clerk of the course, Hugo Beven, has done wonders in the time that he has been there. Unfortunately it is rather a chicken and egg situation — which comes first, the sponsors or the television companies? The television companies like to go where there is good racing, the sponsors like to go where there is television, so it just means a break from one side or the other before a course such as Worcester can really get off the ground.

Just to the east of Worcester, we have **Stratford-on-Avon** which is probably one of the most thriving racecourses in its league, always attracting a large number of paying customers. They are a genuine bunch of racing enthusiasts who regularly turn out to enjoy the racing which invariably includes many Lambourn-trained horses. Stratford-on-Avon has in its head groundsman, Reg Lomas, an extremely hard-working person who has a great knowledge of turf and what is needed to ensure its continued growth is not damaged beyond repair when many horses gallop over it on wet afternoons. It is not just the question of replacing the divots, and that in this day and age with high labour costs is difficult enough, but it is to encourage new growth when the old turf has been cut to ribbons. Reg Lomas can also be relied on to give trainers an accurate assessment of the ground conditions, which is appreciated throughout the industry. The grounds also possess a first-class watering system which is used to produce very creditable results.

Farther to the east is **Towcester** racecourse, situated in Northamptonshire and close to the M1 motorway. Towcester is one of a handful of courses in the country that has an extremely steep hill to finish on, invariably producing results that would be quite different if the same horses met on a flat track. It is owned by the Hesketh family (who have diversified into motor racing over the last few years, providing James Hunt with a stepping-stone to his World Championship) and as a result is always kept up well, with the railings painted, and, to complete its picture-book outlook, when the weather permits, the starter is taken down to his starting rostrum by pony and trap. This course really needs to be known well. Young lads get excited too soon thinking they are going to win, and are apt to 'ask' their horses when climbing the hill. It is quite important to get a good position by the bottom of the hill and then take hold of your horse allowing him to 'idle his engine' as he meets the rising ground. Having saved some energy on the first part of the hill a horse, given a chance to fill his lungs, takes a blow and is able to go again when the runners face up to the second-last fence or hurdle. An enthusiastic crowd attends meetings here.

In 1978 the promotion of the course was put into the hands of local businessman and keen racehorse owner, Ken Weller who has Thames Television presenter Michael Wale as his partner. The venture augurs well for Towcester's future, and likewise for British racing, with plans such as an indoor parade ring to ease the plight of the long-suffering British racing public.

Farther to the west we have **Cheltenham** racecourse, the Mecca of steeplechasing. The three-day festival meeting in March produces the champions of the current season, and it also has many other popular meetings such as those featuring the Massey Ferguson Gold Cup and the Mackeson Gold Cup, held before Christmas of each year. Another attraction is the all-amateur United Hunts meeting which is held in May when the club area is thrown open to the public. The whole racecourse is available for a charge of £2.00 per head, which is considerably less than the normal entrance fee to the club enclosure. Here we have a racecourse that has abounding character, and anybody who has raced there, on horseback or having trained a runner, owned a runner or simply gone to enjoy the sport, will appreciate that the atmosphere at Cheltenham outshines the majority of other courses in the country. Cheltenham has always been way out on its own in the steeplechasing calendar, but has over the past few years experienced many administrative problems. There have been mutterings from the club members for some years about the facilities and organisation. Over the years Cheltenham has changed its shape and is now down to two complete courses. At one time four-mile races would disappear way behind the grandstands, through the car parks, and eventually emerge back onto the racecourse, but now even the original Gold Cup Spur where the race commenced has been abandoned — the start now being on the racecourse proper. As well as the two complete circuits, there is for the two-and-a-half mile races an additional track starting in the middle of the course and joining the racecourse proper at the two-mile start. Having recently completed the rebuilding of the grandstands, Cheltenham is now a showpiece in the steeplechasing world.

Cheltenham's lead in the steeplechasing calendar has been drastically reduced since Ladbrokes, the bookmakers, leased the right to run the Liverpool meeting a fortnight after the Cheltenham Festival Meeting, for they have produced races of the calibre that we normally expect only at the Cheltenham three-day Festival.

I find it sad that so few racegoers ever bother to walk down the course and stand by a fence, and those who do so, rarely go far enough. I am sure if ever they allowed the time to walk deep into the heart of the racecourse they would both see and hear what really goes on in a steeplechase, especially at Cheltenham. The action is often at its best out in the country, and standing halfway down the final hill one can see horses racing at their fastest, experiencing from the ground just what enormous distances can be covered by a steeplechaser in full flight. When he meets a fence on a really good stride and is asked by his rider to 'pick up', the thrill from the ground can be almost as great as from the saddle. Cheltenham has always lent itself to great victories, and equally tragedies, witnessed by supporters of National Hunt racing in their thousands who are always assured of good sport. There have been many unforgettable moments, and it would take a complete book to tell of them all, but pride of place must go to the great *Arkle* who performed with such grandeur in the mid-1960s, almost as if he knew the public had flocked there to see him alone. A bronze statue reminds younger racegoers of the great horse, the like of which we have not seen since, and although as time passes comparisons become harder, we may never see again.

An example of the unique character and feeling that Cheltenham's followers inherit, was portrayed on the day when Terry Biddlecombe retired from race riding. Terry rode in the last race of the meeting in 1975 on *Amarind*, trained by Fulke Walwyn at Lambourn. I personally led the runners onto the racecourse to parade in front of the grandstand when I sensed that the public were going to acclaim their hero, so I pulled my mount *Soothsayer* back, to enable Terry to lead the parade past the grandstand. As he came into view the first cry from one of his fans soon caught on like a fever, and, as one, the thousands of spectators cheered the man, who had for so many years thrilled them with his brilliant riding. It was a moment that nobody will forget who was present that day, and I know it will remain in Terry's heart as long as he lives.

Just to the west of Cheltenham over the Welsh border is **Chepstow** racecourse. It is run by the enterprising John Hughes, whose ability to attract and retain sponsors has done wonders for Chepstow. Many good races are run there, and it is another course that has character. It is very undulating with the ground varying considerably, always being fast down the back straight and wet in the dips. The fences here also vary; those in the back straight seem to be of regulation appearance, whereas those in the home straight are made at a considerable angle. As the

Hurdle race at the picturesque Warwick Course

Above: Race off to a good start at Fontwell Park which has the longest run to the first fence in Britain

Below: The eagle eye of the television camera follows the 1971 Hennessy Gold Cup at Newbury

Above left: Clerk of the Scales, John Phillpotts weighs Bob Champion before a race at Windsor

Below left: Jockey Club official Neil Wyatt, Inspector of Courses

Below right: New Year's Day at Windsor proves popular with the London racegoers

Right: A peep into the guarded sanctuary of the jockeys' changing room

Above right: Senior starter Major Eveleigh raises the tapes for an excellent start to the 1975 Whitbread Gold Cup

Trainer Fred Winter puts the weight cloth on *Crisp* at Cheltenham

Top: Losing punter!
Bottom: John Hughes the inspired Clerk of the Course at Chepstow, Lingfield Park and Aintree

course in the home straight is rather like a switchback, horses tend to run at them jumping off their fore hand, often being unbalanced on landing and paying the penalty. Here the last fence is right in front of the Tattersalls' grandstand, usually providing a battle royal when all caution is thrown to the wind. Crowds very rarely go away not having enjoyed their day at Chepstow racecourse. It is easily accessible, the staff are pleasant, the setting picturesque and it has its fair share of good races.

In the south, there are some very good racecourses within a close radius and in close proximity to Lambourn, now the premier training centre for steeplechasers and hurdlers in Britain. There is Newbury, Windsor, Kempton, Ascot and Sandown, with Lingfield just slightly to the south of them.

Ascot, with its vast stand, was the latest of this group to operate a steeplechase course having been totally flat for many years. It has been well accepted for some time now as a premier steeplechasing course. Though a normal National Hunt crowd looks diminutive when placed in the Ascot stands, the many sponsored race days, such as Black and White Whisky Day, do fill the grandstand to comforting proportions.

Newbury is the truest course in the country because it is almost two miles around and completely flat. Newbury racecourse is a jockey's paradise since there is time and space to put into operation carefully laid plans. Although as applies with any other race on any racecourse plans often go astray through the horse making a bad mistake, or being interfered with by riderless horses. At Newbury, however, all things being equal, your plans come to fruition and usually the best horse wins. Here, as with Cheltenham the fences are perfectly made and attractive to both the horse and the jockey's eye. They are probably the stiffest in the country. By that I mean the birch in them is packed more tightly than on the majority of courses, allowing less margin for error. These two venues, however, represent top-bracket steeplechasing, and quite rightly aspirants should be prepared to jump 'proper' fences.

At Newbury there is the finest example of a water jump in the country. It is situated immediately in front of the grandstands providing the spectacle that keeps people interested in attending steeplechase race meetings. It is a particularly breathtaking sight to see a field of good steeplechasers really spreading over the water.

Ground conditions all over the country vary tremendously with the time of year. The west country circuit, which was noted for starting and ending the season, tends to have very fast ground, but because they are now forced to operate all through the winter in order to qualify for their Levy Board Grants it has rather changed the pattern of racing in that area. The racegoers in the west country go to meetings for the sport and are true animal-loving people. Although for many years it was considered that the west country provided easy-pickings for more fashionable trainers, the situation has changed, the races being as hard to win there as anywhere else.

Of the four courses situated in the west country, namely, Newton Abbot, Devon and Exeter, Taunton and Wincanton, **Wincanton** attracts the highest class of animal. Their Kingwell Pattern Hurdle has become a recognised Champion Hurdle trial which in recent years, the great *Persian War, Lanzarote* and *Bula* have used as their final preparation for Cheltenham. Wincanton also attracts a regular flow of good chasers. *The Dikler* has thrilled the crowds there, as did *Crisp*, the great Australian horse who made his English debut there, as well as returning for other victories, and in doing so thrilled the west country crowd.

As steeplechasing is mainly a winter sport, it is only to be expected that much of it is run in adverse weather conditions. In the last decade, racing has been put off in wet weather on more occasions to save the ground than from the safety factor. In Ireland, racing continues quite often in conditions that would ensure abandonment in Britain. I hope this chapter shows that the 44 racecourses which provide our sport are varied in every possible way, providing a suitable outlet for every type of horse, and also sport for people from every level of society. The stage is a good one.

Jumping Courses in the British Isles

4 The jockeys

The sport and industry of steeplechasing is sustained by a very large number of people — the owners, the trainers, the stable lads, the racecourse groundstaff, etc. In the forefront of all these people are the jockeys.

The jockeys come from many different backgrounds. Some, perhaps, are born jockeys, others have to work that much harder to achieve success. Every year some 400 jockeys will ride under National Hunt rules, and of these only twenty or so will be able to earn a comfortable living from the sport and only a very few will make enough to be able to save any money. The middle-of-the-road jockeys will be around for many years without actually hitting the heights and will barely be able to survive on their earnings. Most will never achieve any real success, but will be succeeded by many more who are prepared to try their luck at this most demanding sport.

Since the turn of the century, only three amateur riders have become Champion Jockeys whilst still being amateurs. Many more though have gone on to head the jockeys' table after turning professional. The household names who spring readily to mind in this category are Tommy Stack, Bob Davies, Graham Thorner, Terry Biddlecombe, Stan Mellor and Tim Brookshaw, all of whom were good champions. The advantages of starting as an amateur are quite considerable. Firstly it means that a person can be pursuing or learning a trade for the future, should race-riding not turn out to be their forte. Secondly, amateur riders do not get paid for riding, so when they are young and keen, people can engage them to ride their horse at a race meeting without having to pay the £20 riding fee that today's professionals are paid. This situation only lasts until an amateur has ridden on 75 occasions against his professional counterparts. Thereafter people wishing to use the services of an amateur jockey when riding in professional races have to pay the equivalent of the riding fee into a Jockey Club fund called the Joint Administration Fund. It is usually at this point that an amateur rider decides whether he wishes to turn professional, or retain his amateur status. After all, it will cost the same amount for an owner to engage the amateur then as it will to engage a professional. Therefore the amateur may just as well receive the money. Should he, however, wish to retain his amateur status in order to still be able to ride in point-to-points or hunter chases, he will remain unpaid.

By the time an amateur rider has had 75 rides against professionals, it will be obvious whether he has a future or not in the paid ranks. By this time he will have a fair start over his stable-lad counterpart who will have been tied to one trainer six days a week, forty-nine weeks of the year. Most of the amateurs who have gone on to be Champion National Hunt Jockey are sons of farmers, or people who are able to support them in the years immediately following their schooling. The ruling whereby amateurs wishing to retain their status and yet still ride against professionals, are paid for, is a good one. It is debatable, however, whether the money that the owner pays for their services is channelled into the best avenue in the form of the Joint Administration Fund. Many people think it would be far more suited to the Injured Jockeys Fund which caters for crippled jockeys, those that are forced to stop riding through injuries sustained from racing, and to the dependants of deceased jockeys.

However, this ruling has definitely stamped out 'Shamateurism' which was quite rife ten years ago when quite a few so-called amateurs were receiving reduced payments 'under the counter' for riding in races. This practice robbed professionals of their 'bread and butter' by virtue of the lower cost of their services bearing no relationship to ability.

Now with the fee having to be paid for those wishing to remain as true amateurs, any malpractice in this direction has been stamped out. Very few people would be prepared to pay the statutory fee for an amateur, and also give him a cash fee when they could engage the top professional in the country for less money. The exception to this rule is of course if an amateur is riding for his immediate family, or is riding in hunter chases and amateur only races. Another avenue from which a good National Hunt jockey can come is when a flat race jockey loses the constant battle against rising weight, forcing him to join the ranks of the jump jockeys, or if that did not appeal he would have to disappear from the public eye. The flat race jockeys that do make the transition and continue their living in the saddle certainly stand out when it comes to

1 David Mould
2 Ron Atkins
3 Barry Brogan
4 Chris Read
5 Bob Davies
6 The late Doug Barrott
7 Bob Champion
8 Willie Shoemark
9 Richard Linley
10 Paddy Broderick
11 Andy Turnell
12 Ken White
13 Gerry Glover
14 Nigel Wakley
15 Michael Dickinson
16 Jockey's Association Secretary Peter Smith and David Goulding
17 Ron Barry
18 Bill Smith
19 Paul Kelleway
20 Brian Fletcher
21 Bobby Coonan

Above: **The field going to the start at Cheltenham Festival Meeting 1963 with two of the all time greats, Stan Mellor (3rd right) and Fred Winter (5th right)**

Left: **Queen Elizabeth, The Queen Mother presenting prize to Pat Taaffe after winning on *Arkle* in 1965 at Sandown Park**

riding a finish. The benefit of flat racing experience is invaluable providing that the recipient can acquire attributes such as an eye for a stride and an ability to continually pick himself up after a physical beating! On the flat, horses come 'off the bridle' in a race far quicker than they do under National Hunt rules, without actually losing touch with the race. This gives the jockey the ability to 'pick his horse up' and to make him run better than his jumping counterpart.

There are many good jockeys who have entered National Hunt racing in this fashion. This method cuts out many years of hard work in a National Hunt stable when exercise must be done daily no matter what the weather conditions, and they can be pretty bleak. But remember that the ex-flat jockey has already served his time, known and conquered the hardships of becoming the one to get the chance and having secured the chance to have grasped it with both hands. Josh Gifford was the last one to become Champion National Hunt Jockey following a flat race career, while the most recent example of a good flat jockey coming into steeplechasing is the Irishman, Tommy Carmody. He rode two winners at the 1978 Cheltenham Festival on *Hilly Way* and *Mr Kildare*, collecting £1000 worth of Waterford Crystal in the process as the meeting's leading jockey. His style was very effective, and as expected, his finish was tidier than

a great many of his colleagues. But how was he to take the steeplechase fences where jumping plays such a big part? Coming to the last on *Hilly Way* in the Two Mile Champion Chase, having given the horse a great ride over the obstacles to that point, the question of whether Tommy Carmody had actually made the transition to steeplechase jockey successfully, was answered. Seeing his stride some way out he asked his mount for the supreme effort that would clinch the race for him, and having asked and received the answer he wanted he was neither left behind nor jerked forward by the propulsion as *Hilly Way* took off fully, a stride early. He was completely prepared for any outcome, losing no style in asking for this extravagant jump. This is a jockey to be watched, his style will be enjoyed for many years to come.

The third and most difficult way to become a jockey, but the way in which most people have to try, is by joining a racing stable as a stable-lad, looking after two or three horses and hoping that the trainer will reward his hard work by a ride in public. In the larger yards there may be as many as fifteen or sixteen lads all trying for the one chance available of becoming the next person to get a ride on the racecourse. A lad must get on with his workmates otherwise life can be pretty unbearable, but he must also be different from them in order to be noticed by his trainer. It is necessary to be clean and tidy in appearance, and in one's work, polite, attentive to every detail, and to show willingness and loyalty to the trainer. Having done these things maybe, just maybe, the lad is rewarded with a ride in public. Quite often it will be on a moderate animal that has 'no mouth' (does not respond readily to signals from

61

A jovial Macer Gifford

Gerry Gracey after a winter's day race

Iron man Joe Guest and son Jimmy

Tommy Stack

Graham Thorner

His colleagues present popular rider Terry Biddlecombe with a memento on his last day's riding at Cheltenham, 1975

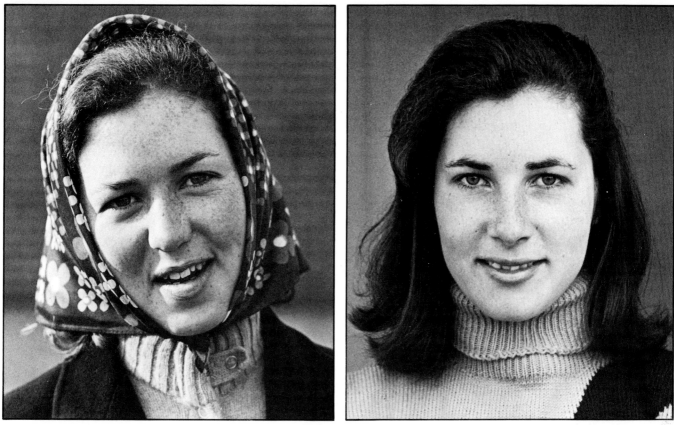

Diana Henderson and her twin sister Jane Thorne who were the first and second lady riders to win over fences, 1976

Mother and daughter Sheilagh and Scarlett French

Charlotte Brew first lady rider to compete in the Grand National, 1977

the rider to stop or turn), or does not jump too safely, or worse still a combination of both. However, if a lad stays in the stableyard he has no chance of becoming established, if he rides even a bad beast he has half a chance. Success or the chance to obtain future rides often depends on a lad's ability to 'play a tune' on a bad animal following a dismal display by a senior rider who may have been over careful in his handling of the situation. The senior rider may have been looking after himself for future good rides, whereas the aspirant is probably prepared to throw caution to the wind in his bid for establishment.

One thing is certain though, when jockeys do attain the status of being established they all possess certain qualities, and you would have to look very deep into the records to find a man who had become an established rider and stayed there for many years without actually being a credit to the human race! Of course, many leading riders possess different attributes, but they all without doubt are pleasant fellows. They know from experience, that when in the saddle they are reasonably safe. If on the ground anything can happen. So it is not surprising in a race when things are going wrong and a jockey is in that awful chasm between retaining his seat and hitting the ground, when only a great deal of luck can save him, then, if at all humanly possible, any jockey who is near enough to hand will reach out in an effort to save the falling jockey from actually going, rather than giving him a little bit of elbow to help him on his way. It is very seldom that a rider deliberately does another one harm. It has been known, but it eventually rebounds on the guilty party. Although no quarter is given, and none is asked there is always the allowable action which is called gamesmanship. I remember, at Newbury when all of us were mentally counting our last three strides going into a fence, Stan Mellor started counting aloud. The result when Stan shouted 'three' was that everybody else subconsciously gave their horse the final kick. Horses picked up from anywhere and everywhere and he did it again at the next two fences. The result was that many horses made bad mistakes, some even hit the deck — naturally Stan won the race. He was persuaded not to do this again by his many colleagues after being held in the cold shower for a quarter of an hour! There is an unwritten law amongst the jockeys that if coming to challenge a rival by taking the shortest way on the inside, it is done with the acceptance that the person who is being overtaken can 'shut the door', ie move over and prevent them coming through. This of course is, in the eyes of the stewards, a breach of rules of racing though experienced jockeys can do it with an air of complete innocence. Early in a race a rider may, if in trouble, appeal to a colleague for some 'daylight' but when the race is really on only the uninitiated or the stupid would venture to ask for a safe passage 'up the inner'.

If a gap does open and it is beneficial for a rider to take the opportunity, he must know his horse has sufficient speed to go through quickly and do so with the utmost stealth. In the 1978 Piper Cheltenham Gold Cup, John Francome, riding *Midnight Court*, used his mount's known acceleration to slip up the inside of Bill Smith around the last bend, saving at least two lengths. This did not affect the result because Bill's mount *Fort Devon* was just about finished at that point, and *Midnight Court* went on to win by ten lengths to provide Fred Winter with a belated victory in the race, the first of many I am sure. Bill said afterwards: 'So quickly did John come through that he was two lengths clear and going away before I realised where he had come from.' There are many young jockeys who would testify that they had assumed the oldest professional riding today, Joe Guest, would be easy meat. Having once tried to sneak up on his inside is reason enough to never attempt it again! Joe is the iron man of steeplechasing, and although not getting the support he deserves these days has never seen 'the red light' and continues to ride, simply because he enjoys it. His son James is all jockey, and would trouble the best if only his weight was a stone lighter. It is essential for a jockey to be a good judge of pace, it is no good going off at a mad rate of knots only to fold up before the end of the race, or, on the other hand, it is equally wrong to conserve energy by settling way at the back when there is a horse with known unlimited stamina many lengths clear and going for home. He will not stop and no matter how much speed your horse possesses you cannot give a great deal of ground away to a leader who does not stop. A good judge of pace must be able to weigh up his rivals' stamina and speed as well as his own.

A jockey must possess a good eye for an obstacle and the better the jockey the farther away from the obstacle he can weigh it up. It does not matter who a jockey is, he will hit the floor or not complete the course on ten per cent of his rides. In doing so he must be able to take pain, disappointment, and often hurt pride, bouncing back ready for his next ride. Racing being as it is, the penny inevitably turns a full circle, eventually bringing the success that makes all the disappointments seem so incidental. Furthermore a rider must be good at public relations. People must like him, it must never be forgotten that racing is to many owners an entertainment, they work hard in their business to earn the money to enable them to have racehorses, so when they go racing it is a day out. Hopefully a winning day, but if it is not the jockey can do a great deal to at least ensure that the owner enjoys his day. Often if an owner likes a jockey, who maybe is not quite the best in the land, but whose company he enjoys, he will probably ask for that jockey to ride his horse again. One fact is certain, if a jockey does not ride horses he certainly will not ride winners.

Top: Ever popular Terry Biddlecombe, former champion now retired

Centre left: Hurdles specialist jockey, Jimmy Uttley winner three times in succession of the Champion Hurdle on *Persian War*

Centre right: Brian Fletcher of Grand National fame

Bottom: JonJo O'Neill the brilliant record breaking Champion Jockey

Top: Diana Henderson first lady jockey to win over jumps

Bottom: Jeff King much esteemed by his fellow jockeys

The great Stan Mellor urging his mount on

Riders in the sauna bath before the Grand National

Of the jockeys riding today, Jeff King is considered in the weighing room by the professionals as their ideal. His great strength lies in his ability to pick-up a tired horse, making it produce its best. That does not mean reverting to the whip. When a horse starts to fade because it is feeling the strain of the race, its lungs are bursting, it is tired. To be able to make that horse forget all those things and still produce a little bit more is a very rare gift indeed. Jeff's strength lies in the way that he can get hold of a horse's head by taking both reins in one hand, pushing from his pelvis and shoulders, urging the horse to lengthen each stride just that half inch that may be enough to win the race. Jeff is a fearless rider, he sees a great stride going to a fence, and if upsides anybody from three out he is very hard to beat. At home he is a very gentle man, a good family man, but on the course he is a professional, and when upset by a sub-standard animal has been known to explain in no uncertain terms to someone who has bred, reared and cared for the horse that it is definitely illegitimate! He undoubtedly has the ability to be champion jockey, but now at the age of 37 his chance looks to have gone, underlining the fact that maybe a little bit of public relations in the past could have helped him along the way. Hopefully Jeff will be seen

riding to great effect for many years yet because he is a fine example of a true professional and does his job to the utmost of his ability, and that ability is the tops!

The proof that a jockey is in the top bracket is when he wins on horses that should not have won on merit. When this happens a rider is said to have stolen a race, and the man to have done so on more occasions than any of his rivals of late, is the record breaking JonJo O'Neill. He is a lad full of bounce. Everybody loves JonJo, and if he has an enemy, I have yet to meet him. He is light, which means that he does not have to diet to achieve the minimum weight, which makes life much easier for him than for many of his colleagues. That, plus his phenomenal success since turning freelance is probably why he is always smiling. JonJo possesses the will to win, which is an important factor in any jockey's make-up, but during the 1977/78 season he has been riding with the confidence that only winners can instill, success breeding success. He does not smoke, he is a teetotaller, and leads a fairly quite life; success has never altered this likeable Irishman.

JonJo has also been the first steeplechase jockey in this country to take on an agent, not to get him rides because they come flowing in by the telephone, but to promote him off the sporting pages. Most other

JonJo O'Neill

John Francome

Tommy Carberry

sportsmen can cash in on advertisements for every day household products, but racing seems to have been ignored. He has now joined the 'stable' of Josie Nicholson who manages Pat Eddery the champion flat jockey, Mick Grant the international motorcyclist, and other leading sportsmen and women from a variety of sports. This is something that is sure to come and has been happening in America for many years, and I think the lead JonJo has given will help it increase before many seasons pass.

Former champion Tommy Stack, the last jockey to partner *Red Rum* in the Grand National, has everything that a successful jockey needs, including all the attributes that we have outlined. He is a nice guy, and is into racing up to the hilt. He knows everything about most horses that are in training, probably having seen them or their dams in Ireland. His

Jack Dowdeswell

Duke of Albuquerque

Lord Oaksey

connections there are the people involved in the grass roots of racing, the breeding of horses. 'Stacky' is not very heavy, and is also a teetotaller. High amongst his qualities is an insatiable will to win. Tommy gets off a horse at the end of a race and is able to tell a trainer or owner exactly what has happened, or more important still, why it has not happened, and what is more he will be right! He was retained by the hundred-winner-a-year trainer, Arthur Stephenson, who constantly claims he is a dealer not a trainer. Tommy is typical of the modern breed of jockey, having an eye to the future by operating a livery yard with the help of his beautiful wife Liz. Fred Winter and men of his era openly admit that they spent most of their earnings each year whilst Tommy still has the first pound he earned — and the majority of those that followed it.

Sadly Tommy has now hung up his racing boots, a decision that never comes easily to a jockey. I say sadly because he will be greatly missed from the riding scene. Tommy has been Champion Jockey, ridden the winners of the Grand National, the Schweppes Gold Trophy and his most recent major race the Whitbread Gold Cup.

In 1978 at 32 years of age, he could see that there was precious little else to achieve, but on the other side of the coin there was an awful lot to lose. With each passing season after the age of 30, professional sportsmen find that their reactions slow up slightly, knocks take that little bit extra out of the body, and the long journey home after a hard day's work no longer holds that same excitement. In Tommy's case, having survived a pelvis smashing fall in the parade ring at Hexham on 5 September 1977, he was able to prove to himself, as well as to the racing world, that he was as good as ever on his return to the track in March 1978. However, the injuries he incurred after his fall have been causing severe internal discomfort ever since. Although masking his pain, it served as a constant reminder that the odds against keeping body and limb together in our sport are poor. So it was, that after five unplaced rides at Hexham a month before the 1977/78 season finished, Tommy realised that he had not particularly enjoyed purely riding around the track with little chance of being involved in the battle for honours. He decided there and then that even though he was sure of several good years at the top, the inevitable decision would have to be made then, so why not now while he was in one piece and still able to provide for his wife Liz?

I for one, am pleased that he has come out with his head high, his mind and body intact and a few pounds in the bank. It is rare indeed for jump riders to finish with any permutation of the above, let alone the lot. He will be missed from the changing room, but a new Tommy Stack will certainly emerge and, furthermore, all the jockeys will move up one place on the changing bench which is the rider's barometer of success.

John Francome, the champion in 1976 and the runner-up for the last two seasons, is in my opinion far and away the best presenter of a horse at a fence that I have ever seen. He corrects his mount with aids that are invisible to the naked eye. Rarely do you see John move when going to a fence, his horses always seem to be positioned correctly when they get there, and I can guarantee that this is not a coincidence! As a result his horses jump economically saving valuable energy which they use for galloping and more often than not they win. Never do you see John sitting back, he only goes forward. John either sits and holds, allowing the horse to meet the fence right, or if he needs correction he kicks for a long one from three strides out. John is also a most likeable fellow who puts owners at their ease before a race when they meet in the paddock. He possesses a ready wit, and although his finishing powers were suspect in his early days, he is a man of high intelligence and realising his weakness, he has strengthened it with each passing season. To my mind he is now a superb jockey.

There are many riders who deserve mentioning, but it would fill an entire book to do so — a selection only have been chosen here.

Because of the danger-element, riders develop a great sense of humour, making the changing room a fantastic place to be. It is akin to the most select clubs in the country, because in order to gain entry a person must qualify for a jockey's licence.

Amateurs and professionals work side by side for ten months of the year, getting on very well together. The true amateurs are headed by Dick Saunders, a joint Master of the Pytchley Foxhounds, he farms 2000 acres, and has retained his amateur status even though his riding would rate him amongst the very best professionals.

Jim Wilson, consistently amongst the winners, is the owner/manager of an equine swimming pool at Cheltenham. Nicky Henderson, for many years assistant trainer to Fred Winter, has now married Diana Thorne, and has set up in training himself.

George Sloan, the American head of a chain of health farms, is a true amateur in every sense of the word. He loves racing, and as a result took a year off from his business in America to ride full time here for the 1977/78 season to fulfil his ambition of becoming Champion Amateur Jockey. George had the majority of his horses with Josh Gifford, himself a four-time champion jockey and now a very successful trainer. These riders though totally accepted by the paid jockeys mix mainly in their own social circle. Josh is a member of a band of retired steeplechase jockeys, who, during their time were the life and soul of the weighing room. Stan Mellor, Terry Biddlecombe, Mick Scudamore, Tim Brookshaw and Johnny Lehane took with them a certain amount of magic when they made their exit from the weighing room, but as one character

John Burke receives the magnum of champagne to celebrate his Gold Cup win in 1976

Jock, one of the many unsung heroes of racing

Mr H. Smith, 65-year-old member of the St John's Ambulance Brigade who man every obstacle on a voluntary basis

leaves another one enters. It is certainly a sad day for a jockey when he retires from the saddle with the realisation that he can no longer enter the changing room — that very select club.

For the past few years the ladies have joined the ranks of jockeys, some of whom have attained a high standard despite limited experience. On the flat there are some professionals amongst the girls, but as yet under National Hunt rules the ladies are still amateurs. Charlotte Brew made history in 1977 by becoming the first woman to ride in the Grand National on her own *Barony Fort*, having qualified by finishing fourth in the Foxhunter steeplechase there the year before. Unfortunately she did not quite complete the course, although she did get to the third last fence. Charlotte took a lot of 'stick' before her Grand National attempt with scribes half expecting her to cause a repeat of the *Foinavon* disaster of 1967. (This occurred when nearly the whole field was brought down in a pile-up. It is generally thought that a loose horse stopped the first two riders, these then stopped the next and the whole thing snowballed causing havoc. There were bodies and horses everywhere and the fence was beaten to the ground by the sheer weight of horses and riders.) Charlotte's mount was never able to lie up with the main bunch which was only to be expected as he had only managed third place in a ladies point-to-point previous to his Aintree outing. However, Charlotte showed she was up to the job by ploughing a lone furrow for one and three-quarter circuits. One year later the brilliant and versatile Irish jockey Tommy Carberry made a basic error which would have sent the world's arms up in dismay had it been committed by Charlotte, but because it was Tommy's mistake nothing was said! Riding the front running *Tied Cottage* who was jumping slightly left-handed over the first three fences and increasingly so over the fourth and fifth, Tommy pulled him over to the right-hand side of the track on the run to Becher's obviously wanting to take the drop at its lowest. In doing so he completely disregarded the warning *Tied Cottage* had so blatantly delivered over the preceding fences. The inevitable happened, fully 30 yards before the fence his mount started to run left-handed and because of the width of the track plus the distance from it when he started his wayward course the pair arrived at the take-off point almost sideways on. Watching on television it was easy to predict disaster, although the precise degree was not possible to assess. The very best that could happen was that the pair had a soft fall without interfering with the rest of the field, whilst the possibility did exist that *Tied Cottage*, faced with such an acute angle to take-off, would refuse or even do a U-turn bringing him into the path of the oncoming horses. Happily this did not happen, he launched himself into orbit only to crumple on landing, happily not doing too much damage to his rider, himself, nor anybody else. As discussed later in the book a jockey is faced with a thousand decisions, the successful ones making the right one 99 per cent of the time. Unfortunately Tommy's one wrong decision was spotlighted by the situation he was in, ten lengths clear in a race watched by a world-wide audience. Had a woman made that same mistake it would have put back many years the efforts of their sex to gain equal recognition in the sport. A woman will ride the winner of a big race before very long as Jane Thorne showed when partnering her father's *Spartan Missile* into second place in the valuable Whitbread Gold Cup in April 1978. The pair went down by just a length to *Strombolus*, who was powerfully aided by the ex-champion, ex-invalided Tommy Stack. Riding the horse that had absolutely buried her at Cheltenham only a fortnight before, Jane and her father walked the course hatching their plans which she proceeded to execute to the letter, and it was by only a length that the whole magical thing eventually failed to materialise. Deciding that the ground was better on the outside and that her horse needed a good look at his obstacles, Jane, who only weighs 8 stone, settled this massive chaser, even though his main intention was to charge away with her. He jumped impeccably and Jane produced him at just the right time. Tommy Stack, who at the third-last fence thought he was beaten, brought all his expertise into play, and quite rightly proved the more effective over the last two fences. But Jane Thorne in her valiant and admirable effort threw out a warning to all her male counterparts, that very soon a woman will certainly win a big race.

Steeplechase jockeys are rather like motor cars, they eventually wear out, and when this happens it is time to retire. The average age for retirement is 35, although Fred Winter went on till 39 and Joe Guest is still going strong at an undisclosed age. When you are riding regularly in the top flight having 400 plus rides a year throughout the depths of the winter, it is a very wearing career.

The actual riding is the enjoyable part of the job. The thrills that a jockey gets from winners or even great jumps on a good horse remain with him until his dying day. It is the other factors that wear the jockey's body out, especially the continual battle to lose weight in order to ride at one's minimum. The things that a jockey puts his body through in order to reduce it are often beyond the call of normal duty. Besides the wasting, the falls, even though some of them do not appear to have caused any damage, all take their toll. Then there is the driving; the 60 000 miles that a successful jockey will have to drive per season simply to get him to his work — a highly taxing part of his occupation. All these factors add up to a high price to pay for one's living.

Even with these facts well known there is no shortage of lads wishing to be jockeys. It is a great life, and any one of the many jockeys who have been forced to retire through injury, would, given the chance, do it all over again! The regular jockeys get to know the officials extremely well. They have continuing confrontations with the Clerk of the Scales over the correct weight because more often than not jockeys are struggling to draw the allotted handicap weight.

There are also many other people involved. The car park attendants cheerfully stand out in all weathers at meetings all over the country; bantering with them continues for ten months of the year as the jockeys try to obtain the best car parking position for a quick get away after racing. There are the men who replace fallen hurdles, who laugh and joke trying to ease the bitter disappointment for a fallen jockey. The St John's Ambulance men, who are ever cheerful, are also in attendance at every obstacle on the race course. They come in for some harsh words from winded or injured jockeys when they are lying in the grass, but realising the pain that their patients are in they quietly go about

their business, even when on the receiving end of some pretty harsh abuse. But at the end of the day the riders are ever grateful for their services, and over the years some pretty strong friendships are struck-up between them.

After the canter from the parade ring to the start, horses 'blow out' quite a lot, they relax and their girths are often slack by the time they have reached the start. It is here that the starter's assistant checks and regirths horses that need the service. Several years ago the powers that be thought that this service was not necessary, wasting valuable time causing races to be late, so it was stopped, but after strong representation by the jockeys and trainers to the Jockey Club the ruling was reversed.

All these people help and contribute toward the steeplechasing sport, making a jockey's life that much easier and making it all in all a very exciting and demanding life.

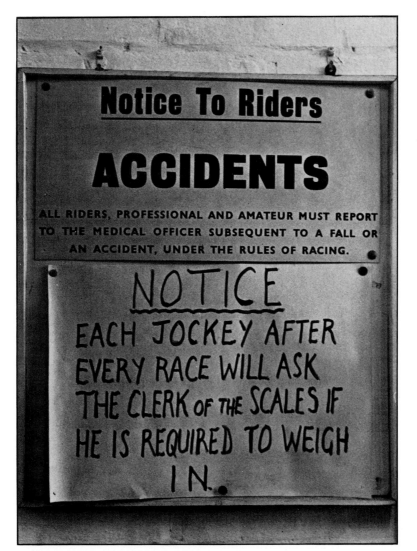

A reminder that an average of approximately 1 in 10 rides ends in the jockey being unseated!

5 Trainers, permit holders and owners

Training is the natural succession when a jockey comes to the end of his career, although not all of them are willing to risk their hard-earned savings to try it. Those who are most likely to make a success of training are the jockeys who have formed lasting friendships with racehorse owners during their riding career, hopefully being supported by these owners when they start training.

The majority of the top-line trainers today are former good jockeys. The four-times Champion Jockey, Josh Gifford, set up training at the age of 28 in Ryan Price's stableyard, from which he gained most of his success in the saddle. Situated at Findon on the south coast, Josh has produced an increasing number of winners in each successive season. He chased Fred Winter closely throughout the 1978 season for the greatest number of winners, heralding his entry into the trainers 'first division'. He is a very pleasant man who is able to get along with any sort of owner which is an important factor for success. Naturally his old 'guv'nor' had a great effect on Josh's methods, even to the extent of leading his runners out of the parade ring himself after helping the jockey into the saddle, thus enabling him to have the last few words with his rider in private.

Josh is a happily married man with two children, and this seems to be a great help. The majority of the successful steeplechase trainers have a wife who plays a major role in the work away from the gallops. Their main job is to keep owners happy, either on the telephone or entertaining them whilst the trainer attends to problems that he does not want the world to share. In some cases trainers' wives go through the sales catalogues marking the horses to be inspected, or they just generally provide a back-up role when things have gone wrong. Josh has never forgotten the trials and tribulations of his own period in the saddle which makes life easier for his number one jockey, Bob Champion, himself in the top flight of today's riders. He is completely compatible with Josh, and I would be very surprised if this partnership does not continue until the end of Bob's riding days, which will, barring accidents, not be for a long while yet.

Bob Champion, in common with many of his colleagues, has always had a weight problem, and as one gets older it becomes harder to maintain the continual losing battle with weight throughout the ten-month season. This makes life very difficult for Bob, and while making the job less attractive for him it does let younger riders in for opportunities of riding the lightweights on the racetrack. Josh's record in this sphere is good, having consistently given chances to his younger riders. At the present time he has four stable staff riding regularly for him in public as just rewards for their loyalty and hard work at home. For the day-to-day work, the glamour of the racecourse is missing and is often replaced by five, rain-drenched hours in which the exercising must be completed. But through hard work stable-lads often win the chance to ride in public. The equine inmates of Josh's stable are a mixed bunch. His owners like the ex-flat racehorses as much as they do the pure jumping-bred animal. Josh Gifford's yard therefore produces winners of all sorts of races, with hurdle races probably just having the edge over steeplechases.

Also training at Findon is one of the growing band of lady trainers, Diana Oughton, who has her son David to assist and ride in public as an amateur. It is probably a coincidence but the majority of lady trainers, at any rate those who do it professionally, are all single women for one reason or another. In the case of Diana Oughton, her husband Alan, who was both a successful trainer and rider, sadly died prematurely some years ago, leaving her to carry on the business he had started.

Auriol Sinclair, one of the longest serving women trainers (she trained long before women were granted licences to do so by allowing her head man to hold the official licence) has never married. She is as knowledgeable as any male trainer and has always been represented at the major racetracks. Undoubtedly, if given the opportunity to take over a leading stable, she would be good enough to maintain the flow of winners.

Also unmarried is Susan Morris, a qualified barrister who has enjoyed considerable success on the racecourse over the last five or six years — 1978 being a particularly good year for her.

Jenny Pitman is in her fourth year as a trainer. She already has many successes to her credit, including the

Midlands Grand National. She has her eyes firmly set on the Liverpool Grand National, and with her representative in 1978, *The Songwriter*, running such a good race to finish eighth after holding every chance before the second-last fence, I think that one day she will achieve her goal. Jenny now divorced, is in a similar marital position to Anne Finch who has been responsible for the training of that good race mare *Grangewood Girl*, who failed by a neck to add the 1977 Champion Two Mile Chase to her many victories.

The west country trainer, Betty Kennard, set up as a public trainer in 1967. She has achieved remarkably consistent results from mainly inexpensive or home-bred horses. Betty has, however, won the valuable Black and White Whisky Hurdle at Ascot with *Fisherman's Cot*.

So it seems that all these ladies have either won a good race or had near misses, and it must only be a matter of time before we have in our midst a very successful female racehorse trainer.

In Lambourn, the 600 acres of communal gallops are used by people like Fred Winter, Fulke Walwyn, Stan Mellor, Richard Head and many others. It is interesting to see that all these highly successful trainers who use the same gallops, employ totally different methods.

Fred Winter is comparatively easy on his horses, rarely letting them off the bridle. He tries to balance the pairs of workers so that one is not vastly superior to the other. The reason being that gallops involving horses of widely differing ability have a demoralising effect on the inferior horse. He likes his horses to set off singly at a fair pace on the real work days, gradually increasing their speed until they reach the last three uphill furlongs of the $1\frac{1}{4}$-mile gallop. The second of the two workers then joins the leader and once together they will instinctively quicken past the trainer who is positioned a furlong from the end of the gallop. Hopefully they will still be nose to nose and really 'motoring' but definitely on the bridle. Fred Winter advocates that it is far more beneficial to a horse not to finish distressed — it should have enjoyed itself, rather than having gone flat out in the early stages of the gallop, inevitably finishing tired and wondering what it is all about. Fred always rides out with the first string, and if he is not racing or has no other pressing business will also ride out with the second lot.

Fred likes to be standing on his feet on schooling mornings, and although leaving the majority of the schooling decisions to his number one jockey he has the last say as to whether or not they go again. On rare occasions, when Fred Winter really does have a trial gallop he invariably rides a good horse himself. Usually leading the two horses which he wishes to work until the real business end of the gallop the workers will quicken by him, enabling him to sit on their tails seeing exactly for himself what is what!

So often when lads are riding at a gallop and trying to impress their trainer they will pass his viewing position with a hold of the horse's head and their nearest boot thrust as far forward as the stirrup leather will allow. This gives the impression that the horse is full of running, when all the time the leg farthest away and supposedly out of sight from the trainer is kicking like mad. This of course does not fool the trainers who have been at the game for any length of time, but it stamps the riders as not the most reliable of work jockeys. Good work riders are rare these days and are extremely valuable to a trainer when trying to assess a horse's capabilities. Fred Winter is in all respects a great man but he has never been too big to listen to his lads' council. The whole racing world was pleased for him when his seven-year-old gelding, *Midnight Court*, stormed home in the 1978 Piper Cheltenham Gold Cup. This race had eluded him on so many occasions when it had looked simply a case of going down to the start and cantering back again. Fred Winter himself always said that he would win the race in time and now that he has done so I am sure it will not be too long before he does so again. His post-race actions are the same in victory as in defeat, so much so that only his closest friends know when he is displeased with the happenings of a race. But each person reacts differently and none can really blame the trainers who do let off steam in public.

Fulke Walwyn whose training establishment is literally 'over the wall' from Fred Winter, prefers to work his horses faster than his neighbour, using the uphill gallop simply for routine cantering. He favours the nine-furlong, almost flat, round gallop for his fast work, using the start of the rising ground for easing up. Besides the difference between the speeds at which they work their horses, the neighbours advocate totally different modes of turn-out for their charges. Walwyn believes horses manes should be expertly 'pulled' but left unplaited when they race, whereas Winter without fail has his horses plaited for public appearances. Both men train their horses to perfection, displaying their 'shop window' admirably as well as consistently turning out a large number of winners each season. Fulke Walwyn has captured most of the worthwhile prizes in his career, many of them enough times to almost call his own! On the death of the Royal Trainer, Peter Cazalet, Walwyn became the principal trainer of Her Majesty Queen Elizabeth The Queen Mother's racehorses and has produced a constant stream of winners for steeplechasing's greatest ambassador. Her Majesty turns up faithfully to see her horses run (state engagements permitting) even in the foulest weather, showing the very essence of a true jumping enthusiast.

A third Lambourn trainer who employs still different tactics is Stan Mellor whose 1000 winners as a jockey will take some time to beat. Always a deep thinker, Stan purchased his present establishment

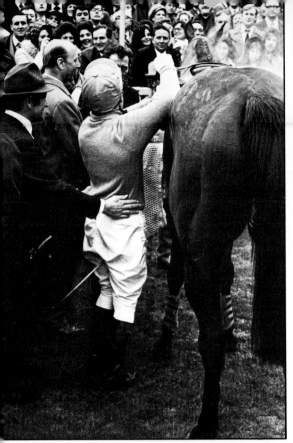

Fred Winter and Richard Pitman experience defeat

Fred Winter and Richard Pitman experience victory

Ginger McCain entertains John White at his pre-Grand National party

Mrs Pat Samuel leads in *Captain Christy* after winning the 1974 Cheltenham Gold Cup

Watchful owners and trainers at Windsor

Left: Singer Dorothy Squires receives the Crudwell Cup

Right: *Easby Abbey*'s owner Mrs G. W. Blow after the 1975 Massey Ferguson Gold Cup

Tony Stratton-Smith, owner, Member of the Tote Board, and Vice Chairman of the Sports Aid Foundation

Viscount Leverhulme, owner and former senior steward

Edward Courage, permit holder and breeder of good steeplechasers

Top: Queen Elizabeth, the Queen Mother being presented with the Schweppes Gold Trophy after winning with *Tammuz* (Fr) at Newbury in 1975

Left: The late Tom Dreaper trainer of *Arkle*

Above: Young Irish trainer, Jim Dreaper following in the footsteps of his famous father

three years before he retired from the saddle, using his record-breaking moment as a platform to launch his present career. He also hired Maj Dick Hern's head stable-lad at the same time as buying his yard, putting him 'on ice' until the required moment. At first he bought a lot of untried stock, but finding that time is expensive has now changed his pattern to include a selection of horses which enable him to have runners, and hopefully winners, from August to the end of May.

Stan financed his own trip to New Zealand three years ago establishing contacts which have since supplied a regular flow of winners. He realises that labour relations are now, and will be more so in the future, of the utmost importance in the smooth running of any racing stable and as a result has tried to minimise the manual work. He has installed two electric grooming machines which are operated throughout the day to cut the time spent at evening stables. A motorised vacuum sweeper has replaced the tiresome daily chore of manually sweeping the acre of tarmac surrounding his stables, and a mechanical horse walker which takes up to eight horses at a time and exercises the animals which inevitably in a yard of any size are likely to be on the easy list. Besides these labour-saving devices, Stan has built a superb hostel which is managed by a top-class couple who provide meals that would not be out of place in a three-star hotel. His method of working his horses differs from both Fulke Walwyn and Fred Winter. Having done similar roadwork, Stan takes his string on 'mystery tours', cantering slowly mile after mile. It has not escaped his elders that he covers two circuits of the round gallop before deviating to the home gallop encircling the schooling ground, ending close to the hallowed flat racers straight mile. Once his charges are fit, Stan does very little galloping, preferring to keep the horses wind right by a work out on Barry Hills' one mile all-weather gallop. This gallop starts only a quarter of a mile from Stan's stables, thus the work can be completed in three-quarters of an hour which in the depths of winter can be very beneficial to thin-skinned animals. In the summer of 1978 he decided to keep his string stabled instead of putting them out for their usual annual holiday at grass. His reasons were that horses at grass become physically soft as well as putting on hundredweights of surplus fat which often takes to the following Christmas to trim off. Stan also believes that we ask too much of a horse, taking far more out than we put in. Although his plans have passed the blueprint stage he is as yet keeping their content 'under his hat'.

A fourth Lambourn trainer, Richard Head, likes to take more time than most to prepare his horses. He keeps them at home until he thinks they are fit to do themselves, and himself, a justice. He would be by far the most sympathetic trainer regarding work with his horses of those mentioned so far. A shy, almost reserved man, Richard Head soon found the worries and frustrations of training enough to warrant the extreme use of his vocal chords on the schooling ground. His approach to the welfare of his charges is a methodical one in an effort to produce the best from the material available. Faced with many training problems regarding his top-class hurdler/turned chaser *Border Incident*, Richard Head has produced him to win eight of his only twelve races. His racing career at the end of 1977/78 season spanned five seasons, giving some indication that as racing commentators are apt to say, the gelding 'has been difficult to train!'

When broken blood vessels plagued *Border Incident*, Richard Head left no stone unturned in search of a cure for this long-standing ailment. Since the recognised medication that was used to prevent this particular malady has been placed on the list of banned drugs, trainers have either tried to find the cause of the trouble or accept defeat gracefully — retiring the afflicted animal. In the case of Richard Head, he sought the advice of all known experts, finally pinning his faith in the theory that dust is the cause of the irritation which in turn causes horses to break blood vessels in their upper nose when under pressure. When this happens the animal is stopped as quickly and effectively as if shot. At first the only sign is a rapid deceleration but it is quickly followed by a flow of blood down either or both nostrils according to the severity of the break.

The hay lofts situated above the stables were emptied, the hay and oats dampened before consumption and the straw bedding replaced by peat moss in an effort to minimise, if not eliminate, the dust intake into *Border Incident*'s lungs. It worked wonderfully, but as so often happens when a trainer manages to stop one nightmare — another starts. *Border Incident* being a hard-pulling, excitable individual puts his all into everything, and as a result he contracted sore shins. To the layman this complaint sounds a little unimportant, although in practice it is serious enough to make a horse lose any shred of form at best and to prevent it from seeing a racecourse for some months at the worst. It is basically concussion of the shin-bone, usually caused when an animal gallops on firm ground, but it can also occur from galloping in really deep ground. Two-year-olds suffer from this complaint regularly since their bones are often not fully formed, but more often than not when treated with a liniment they can resume work within days. It is, however, a totally different story with a fully matured jumper. It follows that because their bones are that much harder, the condition is more difficult to contract and consequently, to cure. It is evident when a horse has sore shins by simply running your hand gently down the front of the cannon-bone, applying increasing pressure to ascertain the severity of the complaint. In severe cases a horse will almost collapse

Jenny Pitman

Derek Kent and Auriol Sinclair

Edward O'Grady

Des McDonagh

Josh Gifford and wife Althea

on top of the person who is feeling its legs in an effort to avoid the handler's touch which it knows will bring acute pain.

Border Incident set the ante-post market alight for the 1977 Piper Gold Cup following a fluent win at Wincanton in February which reduced his price for the following month's jumping classic to only 6 to 1 whilst he was really only a novice. Richard Head was then in the position of deciding whether to run, risking permanent damage, or to withdraw. If they went to the post the combination had some chance of success, to stay at home they had none. He chose to give his charge the time needed to recover — an admirable decision!

Border Incident did recover from his sore shins during the summer vacation, reappearing to record an impressive victory over previous Gold Cup winner *Royal Frolic* at Wincanton, but sadly contracted a strained tendon which assured a further spell on the sidelines. In cases like this where a trainer strives to conquer one setback only to meet another head-on, racing seems unfair and somewhat frustrating.

Richard Head produces a steady string of winners each season, mainly from November to March, and has proved times over his ability to produce a horse fit to win on his seasonal debut. He differs from the aforementioned trainers by virtue of his background, being the son of Lord Head, and also by his comparative lack of race-riding experience.

Away from the training centres, horses are trained equally successfully. Many of the leading jump trainers have their own farms, or rent large acreages to train on. David Barons trains a large string of racehorses at Kingsbridge in Devon on his 600-acre farm which provides his total requirements. The very fact that he can grow his own forage cuts the cost of training bills quite considerably, added to which it provides work for his staff during the close season. Another saving factor is the use of the farmland as gallops, eliminating one of the many 'extras' that appear at the end of the trainers' bills.

Horses trained on a farm often have a fuller, more natural existence. Instead of the same piece of ground to gallop on, farmer/trainers have the facilities to work horses without them actually realising that they are doing so. In some cases they may have to improvise or make do with much shorter lengths of gallop or indeed rougher ground, making up for that with the variety. Nothing keeps a horse sweeter than occupying his mind off the track. Some shepherding, checking the cattle or simply hacking about, generally encountering the numerous goings-on that occur in the daily running of a farm.

David married into a famous west country racing family and quickly earned considerable respect for himself on his local tracks. As with all successful ventures his business grew quickly and before long he was making five-figure bids at Newmarket sales as often as many of the leading trainers, and more often than most. He has had a great deal of success from this quarter, finding that the complete change in environment helps rejuvenate classic flat horses that had perhaps gone off the boil. The very quality of his charges necessitates frequent trips up country to the higher grade courses which involves a high annual mileage and many hours a day away from base, under-lining the importance of a trustworthy head man.

John Edwards is another who comes into this category — a remarkably consistent trainer, he turns out winners from Perth to Cheltenham but for some strange reason never receives any recognition and little credit from the racing Press. He trains in Herefordshire, which though 'close to the Midlands courses appears to be 'unfashionable' as far as the big owners are concerned. John farms a larger acreage than David Barons and still finds time to ride to hounds. Despite his heavy build he manages to waste sufficiently to ride his own horses in point-to-points and some of his patrons' horses in Hunter Chases. Other trainers in the area are Stan Wright and Michael Scudamore. Both are good men at their jobs though lacking any real ammunition of late, but each has proved himself more than capable of producing a good horse when they have had one to train.

Close by is 27-year-old Michael Oliver who comes from a long line of well-known Worcestershire racing men. His father bought young jumpers for £6000, twenty-five years ago, which makes today's prices look cheap. He is an individualist with strong convictions about training, and along with Stan Mellor could have a lasting bearing on updated training methods. Michael puts an emphasis on breeding, spending every

available moment in Ireland seeking out the stock of the stallions he favours. His handling of the 1978 Grand National third favourite *Master H* was excellent and could not have been done better by men twice his years. Unfortunately his work was in vain as Simon Marsh's chestnut gelding's saddle slipped around his stomach on landing over the right-angled Canal Turn, giving his rider no chance of keeping the partnership intact. As well as emphasising the importance of breeding, Michael puts a lot of store in proper schooling — after all jumping is 'the name of the game'. Most of his staff ride schooling which is done over as many varied obstacles as possible including tyres, painted oil-drums and coloured poles, as well as the conventional fences and hurdles. He likes his charges to know how to adapt to any circumstance or surprise, in readiness for their public appearances. He is a man of ideas and modest confidence who in my opinion just needs luck to be with him in order to figure amongst the leading trainers for a long time to come.

Already established and much respected is David Nicholson who trains on his own 70 acres of land in the Cotswolds. A top jockey for twenty years, David earned the title of 'The Duke' amongst his riding chums and completely fits the bill! In common with Stan Mellor 'The Duke' believes that a way must be found to relieve the boredom of a horse if the best results are to be obtained. To entertain them during the $22\frac{1}{2}$ hours they spend in solitary confinement, 'The Duke' has installed a flock of tame pigeons in a purpose-built loft which forms the centrepiece of his main yard. They fly freely from box to box, some even nesting in the stables. Chickens also roam around the yard scratching at the dung in search of undigested corn, again providing a source of entertainment for the horses. To complete the picture, 'The Duke' has four dogs and several cats whose antics along with the lads' radio give a totally different, equally welcome, source of light relief to prevent the horses worrying about recent gallops or races.

Well taught by his father, 'Frenchie', David turns himself, his lads and horses out in impeccable style. Conventional clothes and 'short back and sides' hairstyles are the order of the day. His lads and horses are instantly recognisable and are very much a credit to him. His staff are the neatest in the country and even when seeking fame or fortune elsewhere they retain the hallmarks of his ways. Each person who works for 'The Duke' or helps in the yard qualifies for his stable tie, with the compliments of the boss!

'The Duke' told me one of his proudest moments was when he saw one of his ex-lads Tony Gately sporting his stable tie on television when leading in *Star Appeal* after winning the Prix de L'Arc de Triomphe. Never short of staff David Nicholson gives them all a chance to prove themselves with no fewer than twelve of his lads riding in public in the 1977/78

Mrs McGovern leads her horse *Davy Lad* with Dessie Hughes up having won the 1977 Cheltenham Gold Cup

National Hunt season. This sadly is the exception not the rule amongst trainers.

His horses are nearly all untried Irish bred stock which he purchases from Padge Berry in County Wexford. Father and son still talk each evening on the telephone to discuss the many problems which inevitably arise from the care of 50 racehorses. Though eager to listen to his father, 'The Duke' has long since flown from the nest, but if not in agreement has no hesitation in making his point of view known.

One of the longest and most successful husband and wife partnerships is that of Fred and Mercy Rimell who shrugged off rumours of impending retirement in 1978 to record yet another impressive string of victories. Fred farms 600 acres of rented land in Worcestershire which also provides him with gallops of every description including the now popular all-weather 'wood shavings' gallop. Grounded ever since *Coloured School Boy* ended his memorable riding career, Fred trains his string from a Range Rover whilst Mercy keeps her eye on things from her hacks, *Bucket* and 'new boy' duel champion hurdler, *Comedy of Errors*. Fred has a long-serving staff who know their job and carry it out with the minimum of fuss.

Although Fred has the facilities for every possible type of gallop, he often takes a box-load of horses to

A successful partnership now split up, owner Pat Muldoon and trainer Gordon W. Richards

Prolific winning trainer Arthur Stephenson ('W. A.') seen rugging up in the winners' enclosure at Ayr

a racecourse, to the beach or even to Lambourn. The effort to keep horses in a happy state of mind seems to be a common factor amongst successful trainers of National Hunt horses, even though their methods of doing so differ immensely.

Unfortunately, the Rimell's office was burned to the ground in May 1978 destroying all records and many trophies of their memorable career which, far from finished, boasts among its big wins, four Grand Nationals, two Cheltenham Gold Cups, three Irish Sweeps Hurdles, two Champion Hurdles and singly nearly every other major race in the calendar.

To anyone looking in from the outside, the Rimells set-up seems to be easy-going, but make no mistake when Fred and Mercy see things that do not meet their approval, the culprit is left in no doubt as to his guilt. Not only have they proved themselves by winning top-class races, but they win with every class of horse, adhering to the old adage: 'Keep yourself in the best company and your horse in the worst.'

Good jumping trainers are dotted all over the country, though the big flat race centres attract very few amongst their numbers. Tom Jones always produces a small but select number of jumpers from his Newmarket stable for his wealthy American patrons, whilst others from the headquarters of flat racing at Newmarket use the winter game as a sweetener for their summer racers, or occasionally to give an early season flat runner the advantage of a race over his rivals. The same applies to Epsom; many of the flat trainers use the London tracks for similar reasons but rarely do they treat the jumping game seriously.

An affectionate greeting for *Ten Up* by his owner Anne, Duchess of Westminster

Her Majesty Queen Elizabeth The Queen Mother shows that she is not a fair weather owner

Great rider turned trainer, Fred Winter observes his horses' schooling

Northern Ireland trainer Brian Lusk

Major Sir Guy Cunard, former top amateur rider turned trainer

Harry Thompson Jones, the main jumping trainer at Newmarket

Bachelor Tim Forster trains at Wantage

One definite geographical change in the supply of National Hunt winners in the last twenty years is the emergence of the North of England as more than equal to the South in producing 'firsts'. Twenty years ago Neville Crump and Verley Bewicke were the only trainers in the North who were capable of presenting a serious challenger in the major races. Now 'The Benign Bishop' Ken Oliver, Arthur Stephenson, Gordon W. Richards, Tony Dickinson and Peter Easterby have joined Crump in the leading trainers' list.

Ken Oliver combines training with his long-established Scottish auctioneering firm, and is also a director of the highly successful Doncaster Bloodstock Sales Company. He has attracted to Doncaster a regular flow of well-bred Irish stores which invariably command decent prices. He likes this type of horse to train himself, and achieves good results. Like David Nicholson, Ken Oliver buys mainly from Padge Berry the Wexford trainer and his neighbours. His wife Rhona is as equally involved as Mercy Rimell in the training, both ladies representing probably as high as 50 per cent of the training activities. A loyal Scot, Ken Oliver once rode the winner of the Scottish Grand National and also trained three winners, but sadly at the time of writing has been 'bridesmaid' on no less than four occasions in Aintree's marathon. His standard of entertaining his guests and friends is of the highest degree, and all that he asks in return is a smile and an attentive ear when he conveys his message in an after-dinner speech. He does, however, have ways of persuading chatterers to listen. Halfway through a pontification at Punch's Hotel in Doncaster Ken noticed that David Nicholson was far more interested in discussing horses with the pretty Lady Sarah Barry than taking in his words. Without drawing breath the host rose from the head of the table taking an unopened bottle of champagne with him, walked towards Nicholson and brought the bottle down on his head. When the fizzing stopped Ken still talking, resumed his place to finish his story, and the following day David Nicholson bought three of the highest-priced lots in the sale. An unusual method of customer relations no doubt — but effective!

South of the Scottish border though on opposite sides of the country are two of the most prolific producers of jumping winners in the last ten years — Arthur Stephenson and Gordon W. Richards. Arthur is a man with fantastic qualities, his photographic memory and his endless energy resources being just two. His topping of the 100 winners per season mark is so regular that it is now expected of him. Should he produce only 89 'firsts', racing folk think he has had a bad season. A modest, friendly man, Arthur is in his own words 'a farmer-dealer rather than a trainer' so heaven help the trainers if he ever decides to become a trainer first and foremost! Arthur is totally against publicity (not that he needs any) because of the way

that many journalists run hot and cold. He has found in the past that the Press, in general, are far from accurate in their reporting of trainers' and jockeys' activities. As a result, Arthur does not give interviews to the Press, although he feels sorry that his former experiences have forced him to arrive at this decision.

His horses are trained on his farm and are kept as close to nature as is possible with these well-bred highly strung athletes. He has a man-made lake which is used for both the cooling-off of legs that have heat in them as well as a plaything after a horse has exercised. He also believes in turning fit horses out into a paddock for an hour to stop them worrying as some tend to. Amongst each season's batch of winners are very few contenders for major honours but his horses certainly do catch the judge's eye more often than not.

With 1000 acres to farm and upwards of 75 horses to care for you would think that Arthur, or 'W. A.' as he is known in racing circles, would miss the odd days' racing or long trip to Ascot Sales when he prunes his string, but there is not a trainer in Britain who manages to be present on as many occasions as he does. At home he is always first into his yard every morning and last out at night and makes visitors feel welcome even when they may be calling at a busy time — but one thing is certain, 'W. A.' does not suffer fools gladly! He has been particularly successful in promoting amateurs who seriously want to get to the top and are prepared to do as he says. Following champion amateur Chris Collins, who now events, all his prodigies have done 'W. A.' proud. Peter Greenall took the amateur championship in 1976/77 and eighteen-year-old Geordie Dunn finished second to the American amateur, George Sloan, the following year.

Gordon W. Richards has also come to the fore in the jumping game during the last ten years, training at his Greystoke Stables in Cumbria. He notched by far his biggest success when *Lucius* won the Grand National in 1978, ridden by Bob Davies. His previous major victories were with *Playlord* in the 1969 Scottish Grand National and with *Titus Oates* who won the 1971 Whitbread Gold Cup two years after scoring in Kempton Park's prestige race, the King George VI Chase. During that time he has employed top-class jockeys to steer his charges into the winner's enclosure. Ron Barry held the reins at Greystoke for several years, recording his two Jockey's Championships in the process and has returned there as first jockey at the time of writing. Ron's understudy, JonJo O'Neill, came through the ranks to take the first jockey's job when 'the big fellow' turned freelance, and it was a good thing he did, too, since he became Champion Jockey. On JonJo's departure, David Goulding was promoted from second jockey to take 'the driving seat', a position that he held for one year in which he partnered 52 winners. Accompanying the success of Richards and Goulding was a series of disagreements which in the end led to a stalemate situation, and inevitably the parting of their ways.

David's quiet style of riding is very similar to Andy Turnell's which to the uninitiated often looks as if the jockeys are not trying. David and Andy are sympathetic riders who take their winning chances when they present themselves but on no account will they give a horse a hard race when there is no possibility of winning.

So a full circle has turned with Ron Barry now reinstated as the first jockey at Greystoke for the start of the 1978/79 steeplechasing season. As with many of his rivals Gordon W. Richards was formally a jockey but in that sphere did not reach the heights he has managed as a trainer. He recovered quickly from the severe blow that he received when his principal owner, Pat Muldoon, removed his dozen-strong string of racehorses to Peter Easterby's stable by recording his biggest success in the Grand National. Happily Pat Muldoon also had a good year so everyone concerned in the drastic reshuffle at Greystoke at the end of 1976/77 season enjoyed the sweet taste of success during the ensuing season. Richards uses the vast expanse of ground available to him to keep his horses in trim, and like many of his contemporaries believes in using water both therapeutically and as a mental relaxation.

During the same period, the Easterby brothers have made racing folk sit up and take notice. Over the last two years Mick has concentrated more on the flat whilst Peter has produced such stars as *Easby Abbey, Night Nurse* and *Sea Pigeon* 'over the sticks'. Sadly, *Night Nurse* has been deposed from the hurdling throne, but what thrills await us when the dual champion takes to the bigger obstacles. Hopefully he will show us his worth later this year and will be a hot favourite for Cheltenham's Arkle Chase. So it appears that Britain has now a well-balanced distribution of jump trainers, all good at their jobs and each a credit to the profession.

However, come Cheltenham's March Meeting and Aintree's National fixture, the Irish trainers seem to be ever able of producing a formidable attack on our top prizes. For three decades the late Tom Dreaper was on everybody's lips as a master of his trade. His five Cheltenham Gold Cup victories, four Champion Two-Mile Chase wins, two Hennessy Gold Cups, two Mackeson Gold Cups and one win apiece in the King George VI Chase and Whitbread Gold Cup made him a much respected man whenever he was represented on this side of the Irish Sea. His son Jim took over where Tom left off by winning The National Hunt Two-Mile Champion Chase in 1975, the same year that he sent *Ten Up* to clinch the Cheltenham Gold Cup, but I do not suppose anyone will better Tom Dreaper's record in the Irish Grand National. His horses won the race not less than nine times, seven of which were in successive years.

Many of the Irish jumping trainers are household names in England. Before he turned his attention solely to the flat, Vincent O'Brien produced three successive wins in the Gold Cup, The Champion Hurdle and the Grand National. The Paddy Sleator/Bobby Beasley trainer-jockey partnership was then to be feared whenever they ventured away from home. 'They haven't sent this one for the benefit of the sea air' was the usual advice during their reign, a fact that was both patently obvious and, as far as the home contingent was concerned, only too true. Over the last seven years Pat Taaffe has been a frequent raider to our shores returning as a trainer with the brilliant *Captain Christy* to the scenes of his greatest triumphs as a jockey with *Arkle*. He, like most other good trainers, places a lot of importance on a horse's mental state of mind, using his straw barn instead of a sand-pit to let his horses roll after exercising — a habit that shows the well-being of a horse.

There is far less 'bull' or regimentation amongst the Irish trainers, with a premium being put on the horse itself. Jodhpurs or jodhpur boots are not considered an aid to making a horse go faster, in fact there are no frills at all attached to the training of jumpers in Ireland. But make no mistake their general health and condition is top priority.

On the south-eastern coast of Eire in Wexford, Padge Berry combines his training with a highly successful horse-dealing business. He has for some years supplied a high percentage of horses privately to English trainers as well as having enough well-bred youngsters to ensure a regular prime position in the sales catalogues at Doncaster, Ballsbridge and Kill. Padge's trustworthiness is beyond reproach, which is an admirable quality amongst horse dealers, and his generous hospitality is extended whether a sale has been negotiated or not. His racehorses are stabled in a new barn-type building built on a sand base which provides natural drainage as well as a soft floor, eliminating capped hocks. Several years ago Padge noticed that his horses chose to eat a certain weed when allowed to pick grass on their way in from exercise. He had it identified, analysed and sought advice on its benefits, and as a result has cultivated a half-acre patch of the weed — called comfrey — which is cut and fed daily as an additive to his horses' normal rations. It is attention to such fine detail which brings a trainer out of the bunch and into the 'first division' of the trainers' league. The younger element who are well established consist of Adrian Maxwell, a self-exiled Englishman, Eddie O'Grady and Dermot Weld, all of whom would be only too ready to agree that good horses are the easiest to train, the real test is to win races with horses that have little or sometimes no ability. However, a complete book could be filled on any one of fifty trainers, let alone a single chapter.

As successful as the licensed trainers, are the permit

Fulke Walwyn

Ken Oliver

Fred Rimell

Pat Taaffe

Keith Piggott (Lester's father)

Stan Mellor

Mick O'Toole

David Nicholson makes his point known to his father 'Frenchie'

Long standing successful trainer Neville Crump

Yorkshire brothers Mick and Peter Easterby

Bob Turnell with his principal owner Jim Joel

holders. Every year several pop up in the results of major races to serve as a constant reminder to the professionals that because a person retains his amateur status it does not follow that his or her ability can be taken for granted. The race that seems to be the permit holders' main objective is the Whitbread Gold Cup. Since its inception in 1957 it has been won on four occasions by permit holders, and in 1978 Jane Thorne came close to making it five when her father's *Spartan Missile* went down by a length to *Strombolus*. Many of the permit holders choose to stay as such, even though they would undoubtedly be successful as licensed trainers, that is providing they could deal with other owners. Their numbers are made up from all walks of life with the farming community representing the highest proportion. In many cases they produce good horses year after year from their long-established blood lines, and represent the backbone of National Hunt racing. Edward Courage is a typical example of the more affluent permit holder and has been well represented in the major races for many years now, most recently with *Royal Relief* who won the two-mile Steeplechase Championship twice and with *Spanish Steps* who was a superbly made horse as well as a good racehorse.

The west country has always been high on the list of permit-trained winners with Tim Handel and Oliver Carter probably the best known to racegoers over the last decade. But winners can be produced under the most amazing conditions. Dixie Sleeman who trains in Cornwall exercises his horses under the arc lights of the china clay pits, using the mounds of excavated clay to do his normal exercise. At the other end of the country we have Ken Hogg a Cumbrian farmer and owner of a pony-trekking centre. His best horse *Forest King* was bought as a youngster for 125 guineas with the trekking job in mind. Even when showing promise on the racecourse his duties still included shepherding and transporting Ken to various parts of the farm. In fact these duties were probably a contributory factor to his success. Horses trained in the normal way, as we have seen earlier, need distracting or even entertaining in order to maintain a healthy balance between fitness and peace of mind. In *Forest King*'s case he was doing both without realising he was doing either.

The mauve-and-white check colours of Michael Marsh are familiar to regular racegoers, and his victories in the 1968/69 Whitbread Gold Cup were but just reward for his long and continued support to National Hunt racing. He differs from Edward Courage by virtue of the fact that he buys his racehorses rather than breeding them. His land near Stratford-on-Avon is composed mostly of clay which is not favourable for the upbringing of young bloodstock. Michael Marsh is typical of the majority of National Hunt owners, putting in far more than he takes out of the game. Thankfully he is still prepared to do so despite the rapidly increasing cost of the sport.

To fully portray National Hunt owners would indeed be a lengthy inclusion, suffice to say they are without doubt a sporting bunch. There are naturally those who like to bet in an effort to offset the training fees, but even then the inbuilt sporting instinct curbs their natural feelings when they do not win either as a direct result of a bad riding decision or one of a thousand and one inexplicable reasons that makes steeplechasing a fascinating riddle. The present members of the long-established racing families still maintain their original personal plain colours of their ancestors, whilst the rest of us have to choose computations of them. The Earl Cadogan's Eton blue and the Duke of Devonshire's straw colours have been no strangers to the winner's enclosure. The greatest success story, however, is that associated with the blue-and-buff striped colours of Her Majesty Queen Elizabeth The Queen Mother. Besides the 300-plus winners she has owned, The Queen Mother has captured racegoers' hearts by her regular attendance at the winter sport no matter what the weather. She is definitely not just a fair weather owner and has accepted victory and defeat as well as the heart-rending experience of losing a dear equine pal or two on the track, and has by her very patronage continued to give the sport a boost throughout difficult times. But it is not only royalty and nobility who own horses, the sport has through syndication come well within the reach of the working man. There are many breeders who are in fact only too willing to lease their fillies for nothing during their racing career having them back to maintain the blood line at stud. Registered clubs can now also own horses, as can limited companies, which has extended potential ownership to counteract the relative hardship that the old racing families have endured through taxes and death duties. However, racing cannot exist without the patronage of its racehorse owners who are prepared to take out far less than they put in (in monetary terms). But let us not forget in these times of increased mental pressure the incalculable benefits that winning a race can bring. Indeed, as with training the racehorse where it is vital to maintain a balance between fitness and mental relaxation it is the same with owners, where racing provides the mental outlet that the intense pressures of earning a living demands.

6 The horses

All of us who participate or simply follow steeplechasing owe a great debt to the horse who, unlike man, has little or no say in its rôle. Because jumpers often appear annually from the age of three until they are twelve, we have a better chance of getting to know a horse's character, and consequently of forming a stout friendship with them. Of the 5000 thoroughbreds foaled in Britain each year, it is estimated that only 14 per cent were bred specifically to become steeplechasers. It follows therefore that since almost 7000 individual horses ran over hurdles and fences in 1977, a large majority of them were bred to race on the flat, or came to our shores from elsewhere. In some cases the breeder will have a 'dual purpose' rôle at the back of his mind, but even horses bred on those lines normally begin their careers as flat racers.

Whatever the breeder's long-term plan, they will probably first run as two- or three-year-olds, and then if not fast enough to continue earning their keep solely on the flat, they will either be sold as potential hurdlers, or put to jumping by their original owner in the autumn of their second or third season. These animals form the bulk of the huge annual intake of three- and four-year-olds which compete for that year's juvenile honours or Novice Championships over timber. They will be purchased at the autumn sales at Newmarket, Doncaster, Ascot or Dublin. These sales are the rough equivalent for jumping as yearling sales are for the flat.

Of course the trouble is that neither the pedigree nor the early education of such horses was designed to fit them for the long and arduous career of a specialist hurdler – let alone a steeplechaser. In fact of those foals at least 23 per cent are pedigrees which imply that they were intended to make precocious two-year-olds, running over five or six furlongs. Of the total, 63 per cent are in theory bred to stay a mile or more on the flat, and it is mostly from these that the young 'potential hurdlers' are drawn. Even so, on the flat where quick returns are an economic necessity, few owners and therefore few trainers can afford the time and patience to give a young horse the years he really needs to develop bone, strength and substance. Instead, as we have seen, far too many are asked to race as two-year-olds when they are still in effect immature youngsters. That may do no harm to the precocious

spring-bred animals and the more aristocratic middle-distance ones whose trainers have the Classics as a target — they will probably not be able to race until their second season. But for the bigger, heavier, slower types who might with time have been ideal raw material for jumping, too much racing too soon is all too often harmful. Its effects are apt to be mental as well as physical. Not only are a horse's legs, heart and lungs subjected to the strains they are not ready to bear, but he is also asked to gallop flat out over comparatively short distances instead of being taught to settle and economise on his strength. Only too often flat racers are labelled as rogues when their real reason for lack of enthusiasm is simply that they are unable, through immaturity, to produce what is required of them. How often when a horse is apparently looking back at its rider or swishing its tail must it really be trying to say, 'What do you want, blood?' Needless to say there are miraculous exceptions to this rule — horses whose inborn toughness and courage somehow overcome all handicaps, and still contrive to make them in maturity every bit as effective as any purpose-bred jumper who has been given the steady patient upbringing which is the theoretical ideal. The most famous modern example is the great *Red Rum* who was bred to be a sprinter, or at the most, a miler on the flat. He was bought to win a two-year-old selling race (the outcome was a dead-heat with *Curlicue*) which was over five furlongs at Liverpool on 7 April, nearly a month before his actual second birthday. I wonder what sort of odds the leading bookmakers would have offered as to *Red Rum*'s chances of returning to that same racecourse to win three Grand Nationals, and be second in both his other Nationals. *Red Rum* ran seven times on the flat that first year and was back at Liverpool the following March, where even Lester Piggott's strength was not quite enough to get him home in a one-mile handicap. That was his last flat race, but although he won three times over hurdles that winter no horse could possibly have been given an introduction to racing less likely to produce him years later as one of the toughest, soundest, most resolute, staying steeplechasers there has ever been.

So it can be done, and other far less famous names have come through the mill of premature flat racing to

A newly-born foal — a future jumping star?

Mares and foals grazing peacefully at King Edward's Place Stud

make the grade over hurdles and fences. Some of them are in the full sense dual-purpose horses like *Crudwell*, whose record-breaking 50 victories from 108 races included 7 on the flat, 4 over hurdles, and 39 over fences. No horse since the mid-1800s in England or Ireland has ever got anywhere near his total.

But for everyone who attains even a quarter of *Crudwell's* record, there are hundreds who through no fault of their own are too slow to do one job successfully on the flat, and who partly because of the demands put upon them never develop a physical and mental strength to do steeplechasing, even reasonably

well. These horses are the ones who constitute jumping's biggest problems at the time of writing — the unwieldy glut of slow novice hurdlers who overcrowd the winter programmes and highlight the shortage of sound chasers who are the backbone of the game.

Nevertheless when you come to count the sources of jumpers or potential jumpers flat racing must at least, in terms of quantity, be equal to the vast number of steeplechasers bred in Ireland, though the ratio alters dramatically in favour of the latter when horses reach a steeplechasing age. Since 1946 Irish trained horses

fall-back value as potential jumpers. In jumping, by contrast there are no such rewards at either end of the rainbow. Since the vast majority of jumpers are geldings they have no value at the stud. On the day that *Arkle* won his third Gold Cup he was worth no more that evening than he had been the day before. When the active career of any jumper, however eminent, is over there is practically never another field into which he can profitably be resold, except in *Red Rum*'s case. Because of his world-wide fame a genuine offer of £500 000 was made by a Japanese impresario who wished to exhibit him in a safari park. He was to be in the care of his usual lad, Billy Beardswood, and return to his trainer for the winter months. It was estimated that he would attract enough people within two years to repay his new owner four times over. However, it must be stressed that he is *the* exception, *not* the rule!

A horse's sentimental value to his owner may be enormous but the best he can hope for is a contented comfortable retirement. The wonder is that despite all this and despite the low level of jumping prize money compared with the flat, there is still such a demand for potential jumpers that even unbroken three-year-olds are commonly bought for sums which, providing things go right, would take them several successful seasons to earn back on the racecourse.

Unbroken three-year-olds are usually Irish bred horses, which is one of the main sources from which jumpers come. Of the 5000 thoroughbreds foaled in England only 14 per cent as we have already established were bred specifically for jumping. But there are nowadays very nearly as many bred in Ireland each year as there are in England. In 1975 the total was divided into England's favour roughly in proportions of 60 to 40 per cent, but our numerical lead has shrunk regularly since then, and now the proportions are much nearer 50:50. Of the 5000 or thereabouts now foaled each year in Ireland, there is no doubt that a much higher proportion were bred fundamentally with jumping in mind.

The Jockey Club has set up a committee to enquire how the production of such horses can best be encouraged or subsidised in Britain. But even without such encouragement the fact remains that all over Ireland and to a lesser degree in Britain, brood mares are kept with the specific object of providing the raw material of chasing. Their owners are often busy working farmers and these small sporting establishments usually bear no resemblance to the high-powered scientifically organised flat-race studs which have four-figure stallion fees at one end of the pipeline and hopefully five-figure yearling prices at the other. The jumping breeder has never been able to hope for

have won 7 of the 33 Champion Hurdles with a small percentage of the home trained winners being bred in the Emerald Isle, whereas in the same period 17 Irish trained horses have triumphed in the Gold Cup with a high percentage of the remainder having also been bred there.

Flat race owners should be thankful for this state of affairs because it is one of the factors which makes life so much easier for them than for their jumping counterparts. At one end of the scale successful flat-race horses are worth a fortune at stud, and at the other, even unsuccessful ones may have a considerable

Overleaf:
Midnight Court **wins the long awaited Cheltenham Gold Cup Steeplechase 1978 with John Francome**

Life is all eating and sleeping at this stage

any such rich rewards, and has to wait a great deal longer even for the few he gets. However, probably due to inflation and the non-existent incentive to hang on to excess wealth, the 9500 guineas highest price at the Doncaster 1977 Store Sales was topped no less than six times at their June 1978 sale with the two highest prices being 14 500 and 15 000 guineas. It will be some considerable time — which also means money — before any return if any is seen.

A suitable mare, if not raced and won herself, needs to have decent winners related to her although the occasional freak does come along to upset all the established rules of breeding. Generally, jumping stallions of fair repute command between £200 and £500 for their servicing, although they can be found for as little as 98 guineas. In fact the 1976 Whitbread Gold Cup winner *Otter Way* was sired by a 10-guineas stallion out of an unregistered mare. In my view, however, too many jumping breeders make the mistake of sending a mare to the nearest stallion, or even to the local teaser for the first foal, simply to ensure the mare is a breeder. The result is often a nondescript animal, and a year's wasted time. In the nature of things by the time a horse has established his ability to sire good jumpers, he himself is all too often old, infirm or even dead. One such case is the late *Spartan General* who died in March 1978 just one month after starting the new season which was fully booked.

The potential jumping sire must usually wait five, six or even seven years before his stock begin to advertise his merit. Nor since very few entire horses (ie horses that have not been castrated) succeed over fences, can he often be chosen on his own racing record. *Fortina* and *Manicou* were two high-class chasers who have passed on their own qualities, and *Vulgan*, the most successful post-war jumping sire, was himself a useful staying hurdler. Now *Normandy, Saucy Kit* and others are attempting to follow in his footsteps, with the 1978 Champion Hurdler *Monksfield* being the latest stallion prospect. Although he is not due to retire for some time yet, when he does it will be to the equally energetic though more rewarding career of stallion. If he passes on his genuineness and battling qualities, he will undoubtedly be much sought after by the owners of decent mares. But they and their likes are the exceptions. As often as not the jumping breeder has to rely on premium stallions (well-made horses subsidised by The Hunters Improvement Society) or on comparatively unfashionably bred flat-race sires, whose size, strength and racing record, if any, suggest that they might have what it takes. The Irish stallion owners allow far more mares to each stallion per season — 120 is not uncommon. Due to the later age

Overleaf:
Mare and foal at John Thorne's Chesterton Stud which specialises in breeding jumpers

when a jumper starts his career, as opposed to a flat race horse, it is obvious that an early foal is not quite so important, having at least two more years to catch up on his older colleagues before being broken in, and subsequently raced.

Having chosen his stallion and acquired a foal, the breeder has at least three more years to wait even then before he can hope to see a dividend. The potential jumper or 'store' as they are called, will probably, if male, have been gelded as a yearling and then turned out to grow. Even if the youngster has been born with four well-formed and sound legs, a thousand accidents, diseases and unavoidable injuries which can all too easily cut or destroy his value during those three years present a nightmare. If all does go well, the 'store' horse will either be sold privately as a three- or four-year-old, or be sent to one of the recognised auctions at Doncaster, Dublin or Ascot, or if his breeder is bold or affluent enough he may be broken at that age, perhaps quietly introduced to hounds the following winter, and then either put into training or run in point-to-points.

Any promise shown at this crucial stage will of course greatly increase his value, but the corresponding risks are also great. Quite apart from the ever-present danger of injury, the moment a horse appears competitively on a racecourse he is publicly on trial. If three or four runs go by with no sign of ability he can no longer be what the sales catalogues call 'guaranteed untried'. He has been tried and even if the ability is there just waiting to be revealed, his value will still plummet with every unsuccessful race.

Of the 21 acceptors for the 1977 Cheltenham Gold Cup all but four were bred in Ireland, and the sad fact from an English point of view that has to be faced is that far more successful steeplechasers are bred on the other side of the Irish Sea than anywhere else in the world. Blessed with a perfect temperate climate, wonderful grass all the year round, and the limestone soil which is the foundation of good strong jumping bone, the Irish have brought the whole long difficult process of breeding, rearing and selling these scarce, much sought-after beasts to a fine art. To begin with they have a reservoir of proven jumping blood together with a constant supply of mares in whose veins it is plentiful. They spare neither trouble nor money to acquire likely jumping stallions, and the whole slow expensive business is made far more attractive than in this country by a more lenient system of taxation, which recognises the racehorse as a valuable part of Ireland's export trade. Things have changed dramatically over the last few years. Now, Ireland's hurdlers are beating ours, and what's more frightening is that Irishmen are buying their own horses at the sales to take back to race.

Irish breeders have another great advantage in having 'the bumper' race — a two-mile flat race

Jane Thorne with some 'store' jumpers at her father's Chesterton Stud

Young store horses at the Chesterton Stud

confined mostly to horses that have not won and to amateur riders. Appearing in these contests, usually the last race on a jumping programme, four-, five- or even six-year-olds who have spent a quiet well-fed childhood are not over-strained as ours so often are by having to compete with seasoned flat-race-bred rivals. Admittedly the value of form in bumpers is often hard to estimate, and in the results there may occasionally be an element of 'you scratch my back, and I'll scratch yours'. But the young potential jumpers learn to race in them against rivals of similar breeding and background; they learn without the risk of injury involved in a crowded novice hurdle, and when a suitably bred horse of the right make and shape has 'won his bumper', any would-be purchaser from England had better be ready to talk in five figures. There are to be twelve such bumper races introduced in England in the 1978/79 season which along with some more fillies-only races will hopefully ease the congestion in the overcrowded novice hurdles. This indicates in itself the recognised fact that a gelding is far more suited to the arduous life of a steeplechaser, but in saying that I must point out that there have been some very good race mares. The best of them probably being *Kerstin* who won the Cheltenham and Hennessy Gold Cups for Verley Bewicke in the late 1950s. Other top-class mares of recent years have been *Flying Wild* and

Glencarrig Lady, but ominously although they have bred winners none have produced a horse anywhere as good as they themselves were on the racetrack. When venturing to Ireland on a buying mission, it is advisable to be on your guard against the cheerful and generous hospitality which is an integral part of the horse dealing in the Emerald Isle. A couple of glasses of the hard stuff, especially if repeated throughout a long and busy day, can make very ordinary horses look like champions, and astronomical prices sound like bargains. But that is all part of the game and to do them justice the Irish do, occasionally, allow top class prospects to slip away across the sea. Although when Cheltenham comes around they often seem to find one or two left at home who are good enough to beat the exiles. In England and Ireland alike, one route to the top of the steeplechasing tree has always laid through the hunting fields and point-to-points. These of course are no longer what their names suggest. No point-to-point nowadays is run from steeple to steeple, across natural hunting country. There is, however, a fast-developing craze at the moment for 'team cross-country races' which though basically run against the clock sometimes come pretty close to what old-fashioned point-to-points must have been like. But the modern version staged by the local hunt of the area is often an important aid to its finances and is really just a miniature steeplechase for horses which have been regularly hunted, a pretty elastic definition in some parts of the country.

The fields now contain quite a proportion of old experienced chasers, sometimes pretty distinguished ones pensioned off to act as school-masters for inexperienced riders. The most recent and prolific winner of late to revert to point-to-pointing as a form of retirement, and also to educate his new owner/rider, is the 1975 Cheltenham Gold Cup winner *Ten Up*. In my opinion this is a thoroughly good way of giving a horse an enjoyable retirement, as is the hunting field. Some people think it is a shame to see a Gold Cup winner in these circumstances, but for the horse that has been used to living like a king all his life he is still doing to a lesser degree that which he knows inside out, and as a reward enjoys the luxuries of a warm stable throughout the winter, regular exercise, the best clothing money can buy and good food.

Quite a number of sporting farmers buy good young horses for themselves or their children to ride without any intention of going beyond the sphere of point-to-points and hunter chases. Hunt races are also used, part as nursery, part as shop window, by some of the breeders of, or dealers in, potential jumpers. *The Dikler* is perhaps the most distinguished recent graduate, although having run out in two of his point-to-points he can hardly be said to have graduated with honours. *Halloween* was another who moved into the highest class. *Freddie* went desperately close in two Grand Nationals, whilst *Otter Way* and *Royal Toss* also from the point-to-point field both won Whitbread Gold Cups, and any trainer on the look-out for a chasing prospect must be tempted by five- or six-year-olds good enough to win or even run well in an open point-to-point. Prize money in these races has been for many years rigidly limited to £50 by The Jockey Club, but as from February 1979 the maximum prize can be £100 at the discretion of the organising hunt. I feel that the main criticism of the current point-to-point scene is that the fences are apt to be too small, too soft and generally too easy, encouraging horses to take chances which would be fatal over regulation fences.

This situation has also come to the notice of the Jockey Club and some degree of uniformity is being sought as is a seven-pound weight allowance for five-year-olds (the youngest age a horse is eligible to compete in point-to-points). It has not been entirely unknown for 'professional' pointing men to run nice young horses without their lead cloths, (up to three stones) so that they can gain the necessary experience without the resultant strain. However, anybody who uses this method of educating a young horse must ensure that they do not finish in the first four places, otherwise they will be by rule required to weigh-in at the same weight that they weighed out, of course this would be impossible, embarrassing and possibly expensive.

For these and other reasons it does not necessarily cheer a jockey up all that much if when he arrives in the paddock to ride an unknown horse, the owner or trainer tells him confidently: 'He was hunted last season very hard, and jumped brilliantly in our members' race.' The meaning and value of 'Hunted hard' can vary enormously depending on who it was who did the hunting. Introducing a young green horse to the field, strange sights, sounds and obstacles is a task for a strong brave experienced sympathetic horseman. In his hands hunting can be a marvellous education, teaching the beginner to be bold but not foolhardy, cautious and ready for anything, but not faint-hearted. On the other hand for a young horse badly or rashly ridden, the excitement of un-accustomed company, the sight and sound of the hounds themselves, the whole electric, busy atmos-phere, can very easily add up to an explosive dangerous cocktail. If he jumps at all it may be either a disaster or a frightening mystery, leaving him with little or no idea how he got from one side to the other. Riding horses with that kind of background in a steeplechase is no sensible man's idea of fun, but the fact remains that with the right rider a horse can learn many lessons about hunting which will be invaluable on the racecourse. Often dubious riders are labelled as 'only huntsmen', but this term should really be used as a compliment because true hunting men ride and jump obstacles that many licensed jockeys would ask for a bonus to even attempt.

England and Ireland are not of course the only countries where potential jumpers are produced. Many good ones, mostly hurdlers, have been bought in France, although nowadays the high level of prize money there for jumping as well as for the flat is apt to force the prices pretty high. The late Peter Cazalet and Ryan Price had great success with French-bred horses, the immortal *Mandarin* came from France, and David Morley has lately used the French market also with success.

There is little jumping in America and this is largely because the punters there do not like to see their money in the air. Many rich sporting Americans therefore come to race in the British Isles. The American horses, however, that have been sent over to this country have a formidable record. *Jay Trump* graduated brilliantly from the timber of the Maryland Hunt Cup to the very different, though equally formidable obstacles of the Grand National. He would almost certainly have won the Grand Steeplechase de Paris too, if his rider Tommy Smith had not been forced to waste so hard to do the weight. *Fort Devon* though admittedly bred in Ireland and an unsuccessful point-to-pointer in his early days, is another Maryland Hunt Cup winner to make his presence felt over here. He has not yet run at

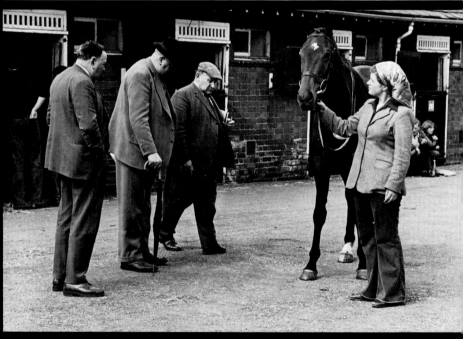

Above: The champion shows he has character

Top right: The four-year-old supreme champion at Doncaster pre-sale show, sponsored by Philip Cornes, who fetched 15 000 guineas the next day

Centre right: Careful inspection by prospective buyers at Doncaster sales

Lower right: Early viewing of the bloodstock

The sales ring

Goff's new bloodstock sales building in Eire with Managing Director Jonathan Irwin

Trainer Ken Oliver in a different role

Winning Grand National jockey John Cook displays his
goods at the Old Ascot sales

Aintree, but time may show that the big fences have no problems for him, too.

American jumping enthusiasts have for the past six years staged the Colonial Cup in South Carolina. It is an international steeplechase to which the best jumpers in the world are invited. Until last year the home defence had been more than adequate to beat all comers, but in 1977 *Grand Canyon* came around the world from his birthplace in New Zealand, via England, Italy and France (he won races in all three) to become the first-ever foreigner to take the Colonial Cup. Although 'a dry' state, the hosts in their usual generous manner obtained a crate of Guinness especially for Harry Foster, the man who travelled with and looked after *Lanzarote*, when he tried his hand there. Unfortunately the hosts underestimated Harry's drinking capabilities, and the crate only lasted for three days!

Before *Grand Canyon* appeared, *Crisp*, the horse who failed by only three-quarters of a length to give *Red Rum* an incredible 23 lb in the 1973 National, demonstrated memorably the toughness and adaptability of horses from down under. *Crisp*, now happily retired and hunting in Yorkshire, was bred in Australia, but since then New Zealand has come right to the fore as a brand-new reservoir of jumping talent. There are, as Stan Mellor and Derek Kent have discovered, certain special problems involved in bringing horses from one side of the world to another, mainly caused by differences of climate and surroundings.

The best time to import horses from New Zealand is at the end of their summer in March or April, then they arrive in this country with our summer still to come, and should be reasonably well acclimatised before the new jumping season begins in the autumn. Needless to say not all New Zealand-bred horses have anything like *Grand Canyon*'s power and versatility, but in many cases their outstanding qualities include soundness and ability to act on hard ground. In a dry autumn or spring many home-bred jumpers hate the hard ground, and especially at the start of their careers can only be raced on it at considerable risk. It is at such times particularly that the tough durable New Zealanders are a priceless asset to a trainer. But because of the cost of travel, prices are now on a par with those in Ireland, and for the money they need to be more than just top-of-the-ground early and late-season horses.

But wherever you go in search of new talent, what should you look for? Is there an ideal jumping type, and if so which are the most important qualities? You would of course get almost as many different answers to these questions as there are people looking for horses, but here briefly and very much open to argument are mine.

Your first impression of the horse must surely come at the top of the list. His courage, character, intelligence and enthusiasm for the game will only be proved when he starts to race, but you can look for clues. An attractive head, a bold eye and a general look of eagerness and interest in his surroundings. There are exceptions of course, but not many good brave horses have small piggy ears. Size is a matter of taste, but as Stan Mellor says with feeling, 'They must at least look big and strong enough to stand the racket.' A British jumper will sooner or later have to carry twelve stone or more for a minimum of two miles, so in the nature of things a lightly-built 'weed' is unlikely to last very long. On the other hand exceptional size can be a mixed blessing. It may be true that good big ones beat good little ones, but the heavier the horse the more strain on his legs, and the longer his stride the more difficult he may find to solve the problems of jumping at speed. Also the ever-present danger with over big horses is that they will contract leg or wind trouble, or worse still, both, rendering them useless. Again there are exceptions, for example one of the 1978 top two mile novice chasers *Space Project* was hobdayed (an operation on the throat to improve a horse's breathing) as a yearling, and has since undergone a similar operation again as well as being tubed (a metal tube is inserted directly into the windpipe) twice. Tubing has been unpopular for some ten years now, but seems to be making a comeback of late. The 1978 Topham Trophy victor, *Canit*, is another which has been hobdayed, tubed and also fired (his flexor tendons have been contracted by the use of red hot firing irons), but it has not stopped him. Whatever his size he must ideally be an athlete, balanced, agile and well co-ordinated. If buying at the sales you are unlikely to see a horse do more than walk and trot, but even then the clues are there. Does he move straight and use himself? Do his hind feet at the walk fall well ahead of the front ones? In a really good walker they should do so by several inches, and his trot should be an easy swinging bounce with his toes thrown forward, landing light as though on springs. Again, and luckily for buyers from all wealth brackets, not everybody has the same idea of what constitutes a good horse. An example is the chestnut *King or Country* which was on sale in Ireland for over three months with many of the top English trainers looking at him but all taking a dislike and not purchasing. Eventually *King or Country* was bought by David Barons the West country trainer, and since has won twice at Cheltenham, including the National Hunt Festival Meeting, and also at the Aintree meeting leaving many of the early viewers with a sour taste in their mouths.

When galloping and even more when jumping, a horse's fore legs are subjected to greater more constant strain than any other part of his body. They are therefore the first place you look for any sign of weakness. The expression 'good jumping bone', really means a cannon-bone, thick and strong enough to

support the vital main tendon and suspensory ligaments which run down behind it. A horse is said to be 'back at the knee' if a line dropped straight from his knee would fall behind the centre of his fetlock joint. He is unlikely on that evidence to stand the strain of jumping for any length of time. His pasterns, the sloping bones below the fetlock or ankle, are as vital as the shock absorbers of a car. They should not be too long or too sloping, but above all not too perpendicular. Timmy Hyde one of the most successful producers of youngsters in Ireland says he forgives several faults in a horse but not bad legs, particularly the fore legs. He looks at the individual first and then at his breeding, and never buys a horse that he does not like, even if it's bred well enough to be able to catch racing pigeons.

As for the feet, large ones do not necessarily mean their owner will be able to gallop through the mud. His action, strength and weight may be just as important, but small 'boxy' feet are pretty sure, sooner or later, to give both the blacksmith and the trainer nightmares.

A 'good front' means a powerful sloping shoulder, and enough depth through the girth to give room for heart and lungs. A line drawn from the top of the withers to the front of the chest, should slant at an angle and not straight down towards the fore leg. The best way to judge this feature is to sit on the horse yourself, and riding one with a bad front feels like someone perched on the edge of a precipice.

Showring judges make a good deal of fuss about hind legs and obviously they combine with the hindquarters to provide vital motive power both for galloping and jumping. But as long as the hocks and second thighs are strong, it does not seem to me to matter all that much if the hind leg is not as straight as a purist might demand. For every horse who goes wrong in his hind leg at least 100 more break down in front. But all this is very much a matter of personal opinion. Great judges are probably born as much as made, and they may often ignore the rules and trust the priceless instinct which tells them that the horse has what it takes. After all provided his conformation allows him mechanically to gallop and jump, the truly important qualities are mostly invisible — that is character, courage, intelligence and willingness to run, without which all the good looks and physical strength in the world are of little use.

Jumpers come in all shapes and sizes, and as we saw with *Red Rum* their pedigree can be hopelessly misleading. Obviously some trace of established jumping blood is an advantage, and a proven pedigree is certainly highly relevant to an untried horse's value. But although a few great brood mares and female lines and stallions do keep churning out the winners, the sad expensive fact remains that lightning does not all that often strike the same place twice. A horse may be full brother to a champion, but it will not make him go any faster if his blue-blooded frame happens not to contain an engine of comparable power.

But at the end of the day the man who writes the cheque determines the value of a young horse and, thank goodness for the health of the industry, people accept or reject different faults, thus ensuring that they all find a home.

Left:
A light-hearted moment for trainer's son Arthur Moore and *L'Escargot* after winning the 1975 Grand National

7 Training

Having travelled much of the country and seen horses trained in widely varying fashions, I have come to believe that there is no one real secret behind the most successful of trainers. However, it is apparent that in all cases where the winners flow year after year there are several common denominators.

It is not always the trainers who have the highest number of winners who are the best trainers. In fact I am sure that there are many cases of animals from big yards who being transferred to smaller establishments would undoubtedly improve due to the amount of individual attention they could receive in comparison to that given to them in the bigger stables. Over the years there are trainers who consistently turn out winners and this of course can be no fluke. I personally feel that a good trainer is one that comes to the fore and turns out a high percentage of winners from runners even though his or her name may not figure as the trainer of major race winners.

It is undoubtedly an arduous task to be a National Hunt trainer, one reason being that the bulk of the work has to be done through the dead of winter when conditions are not just bad, but often desperate. They are seemingly on call 24 hours a day, and are concerned not only with the welfare of their horses but the daily lives of their stable staff. Many trainers when asked what is the most difficult part about training racehorses will pause and then answer, 'Training their owners.' Owners as with every other section of the National Hunt scene cannot be bracketed together; they come in all shapes and sizes and from all walks of life. Having bred or bought a horse and paid the costly weekly training fees, usually boosted by many additional expenses, they naturally like to get some return from their money. Because National Hunt horses run only eight times a season on average, there are long gaps to be filled between races, so if allowed to do so they ring up daily to discuss their horse's progress with the trainer. However, if one is training 60 horses for 45 owners, or as is the case these days with increased syndication, 60 horses with 90 owners, one just does not have the time. Generally, however, in the cases of syndication where as many as 12 people may own one horse, one man usually acts as their spokesman. He does all the arranging with the trainer,

relating the plans to his syndicate members himself. When syndication was first allowed by the Jockey Club it was totally abused by several heads of syndicates to such a degree that several of them received long spells of suspension from the racetrack. But a little good usually comes out of every bit of evil, as in this case. Now after extensive thought, the whole spectrum of syndication seems to be watertight as far as malpractice is concerned, with audited accounts required for inspection annually.

Over the last decade it has become more and more popular for trainers not to break in their young stock themselves. Instead they send them to one of the many professional livery yards where time may be devoted to this very important part of a horse's training. A lot of importance is attached to the breaking in of National Hunt horses because many of them will have attained the age of four before being asked to obey any instructions from a human being. This often comes as a shock to a large, strapping Irish-bred thoroughbred who for the previous four years has wandered totally free in lush pastures only having to worry about the daily filling of its stomach. When breaking in it is easy enough to work a horse on the lunge rein until it is almost 'legless' — tired beyond retaliation point. A rider is then thrown on board. This is not good enough, even though the end result may have been achieved. When mounting a tired horse most competent riders could stay 'in the plate', although the moment the horse regained its strength it would undoubtedly try to put the rider on the ground. His 'mouth' would not have been formed and as a result it could cause grave concern in later years to any jockey when the horse paid scant attention to his desperate tuggings on the reins to get out of trouble approaching an open ditch.

It is preferable, though not necessary, to have an enclosed space when attempting to break in a young horse. This is because the enclosure will do half the work for the person who is doing the job, since the boards, or whatever else are used to form the enclosure, will force the horse to go in a circular path around the handler without undue pressure being used. Having run wild for its entire life everything is strange in these new surroundings. At all times kindness must be used although any disobedience must be corrected firmly before bad habits develop.

Initially the young horse is led around the roads with a bit in its mouth, which surprisingly they accept with little or no fuss. They are often left in their stables with the bit in their mouths so that they can play with it during the day, getting used to it and in turn hardening the corners of their mouth. Having led the horse, and it may be necessary for a second person to follow him just to ensure that he does go in a forward direction, the horse will be taken to a suitable place for lunging. The corner of a field where two sides are enclosed by natural hedges is suitable, but in the case illustrated Jenny Pitman can be seen in the days before she became a racehorse trainer, when she had a Livery Yard, using her indoor school.

She first makes friends with the animal who is to be broken in. A roller is placed around the horse's middle which is at first totally unacceptable to them, but after bucking and kicking and finding they cannot dislodge it they eventually accept it (some taking longer than others).

The horse is now ready, having a bit in its mouth and a roller around its middle, to be lunged in a circular fashion around the handler. The lunge rein is not attached to the ring of the bit in order to pull the horse round but is attached to a ring on the nose piece of a cavesson bridle in order to get the horse to circle the handler without its mouth suffering from any undue pressure. It is vitally important that the handler makes the horse in question go in either direction around him. Only too often horses are lunged in one direction purely through laziness, having the desired effect of 'getting the horse's back down', but in turn teaching it to lead with only one or other of its fore legs. In nearly every case where a horse has been broken quickly, it will lead with its near fore indicating that it has been lunged only in an anti-clockwise direction. In its later training it will become apparent that the horse was only trained in one direction, and if strong-minded enough will become difficult to handle both on the training grounds and racecourses that do not go in the direction that the horse favours.

Horses, as with many other animals that are trained by humans, respond well to the handler's voice — the tone indicating either pleasure or displeasure with the horse's actions.

When lunging in either direction for several days has been completed to the satisfaction of the handler, a saddle will replace the roller on the horses back, a second rein will be attached to the cavesson and these reins threaded back through the stirrup irons and taken behind the horse's hindquarters. When this has been done successfully in either direction the handler will drive the horse from behind, holding a rein in each hand and orally give instructions to the animal to walk on, halt, or to turn, and at the same time make the appropriate physical aids by means of pulling on the reins.

When, as in the case illustrated, the horse will go in and out of small oil drums, walk over poles and completely satisfy the handler that its mouth is responding to the human touch via the reins then, and only then will the horse be driven on the public highways. Again it must be remembered that a horse is stronger than a human being so the handler should always walk slightly to one side of the animal in order to pull its head around should they come across startling objects. Once a horse takes fright there are few, if any, men who could stop them taking charge if directly behind the horse's hindquarters.

Having driven the horse on the roads for a day or two satisfactorily, and encountered many new hazards the handler will then seek further help in order to 'back' the horse. This must be done very gently remembering that it is totally alien to the young horse to have anything on its back at all. One thing is for certain — anything that it may have had on its back in the previous four years, would not have remained there for long! When the rider is legged on to the saddle for the first time, he simply lies across it and is led around until the horse shows signs of acceptance of this burden. The handler will be able to determine when the horse has accepted the weight on his back by the animal's general condition. He will settle down and no longer look back at the rider. It is then time for the rider to be legged completely into the saddle where he must sit as still as possible. Any quick movement or unexpected contact between the rider's boots and the horse's side will cause the horse to react violently. The handler will be constantly talking to the horse, giving it odd titbits when deserved throughout this process. In my considered opinion a reliable person at the head of the animal is imperative, it is probably even more important than the rider. If a horse objects to the rider and starts to plunge off, he will be in dire straits if the handler should let go of the controlling rein. The ensuing five minutes would be extremely tense, even uncomfortable, for the man on the horse's back as the horse tried every trick in the book in order to get rid of the alien. Horses that have broken loose from their handlers often try to get down to dig holes in the floor or rub their riders off against the sides of the enclosure.

Once the rider is safely installed on the horse's back it is far from plain sailing, and he will probably need to be led in both directions for some time before riding on his own. Once the stage of acceptance has been reached successfully, horses will pick up their commands quite readily, acknowledging their new subservient roles. The rider must take over where the handler leaves off, still using oral instructions whilst giving physical aids.

If the premises boast the luxury of an indoor school many things can be done to further the horse's education before it is sent back to the trainer to be

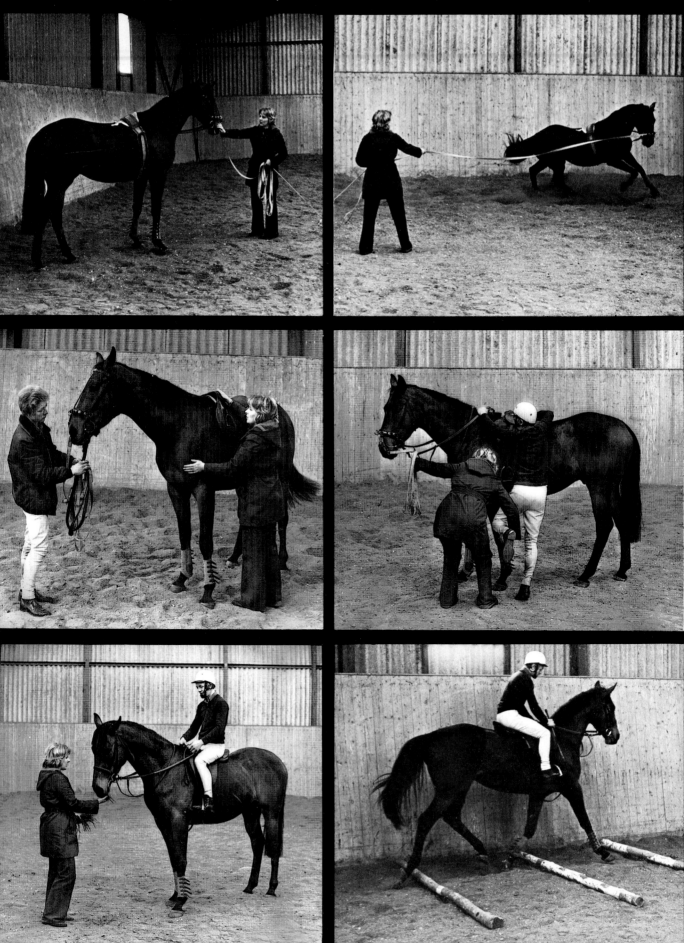

Jenny Pitman breaks in a young horse with rider Bryan Smart

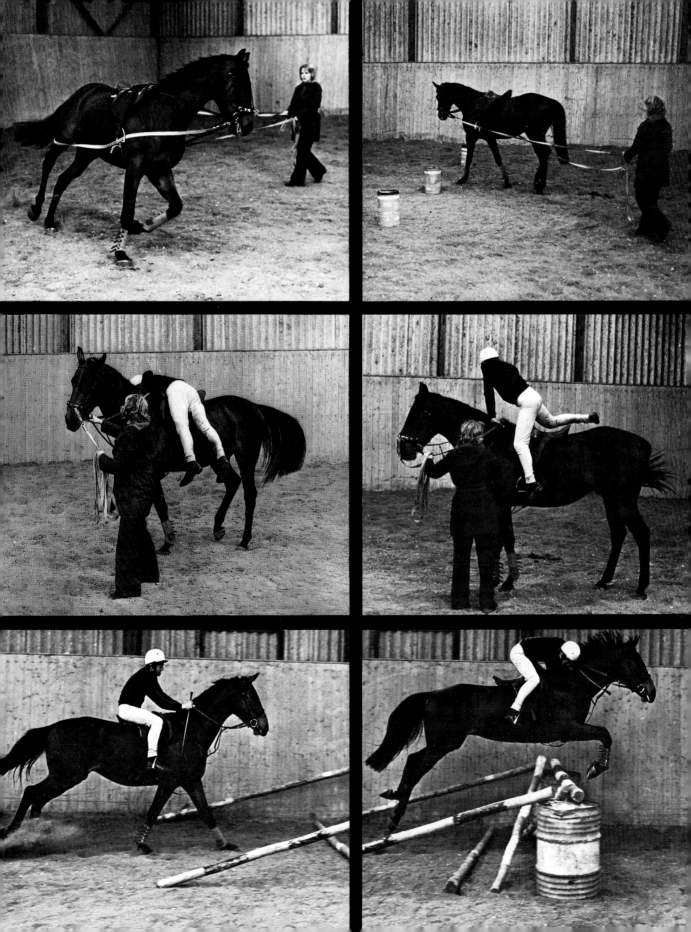

Red Rum and *Glenkiln* galloping on the Southport Sands
before the compulsory wearing of helmets at exercise

The unusual location of Ginger McCain's Southport stable

trained as a racehorse. Trotting over simple poles placed at equal distances apart from each other is a very good exercise in making the horse drop his head to look at what he is doing, thus starting to utilise and control his own actions. When this is done it will be very helpful to the trainer if the handler or rider can get the horse to jump small obstacles. Although jumping comes naturally to a horse in its wild state, with a rider on its back it is at first not too sure what is required of it. Again after a very short time of being shy of the obstacle, but being made to jump it, the horse will readily accept its rider's instructions and will soon be jumping fluently, even looking for the next jump. An indoor school, or for that matter an outdoor school, is not entirely necessary for the best results when breaking in a youngster, it just makes the job easier by virtue of eliminating the distractions of an open space.

Trainer McCain

McCain's string benefiting from the close proximity of the sea

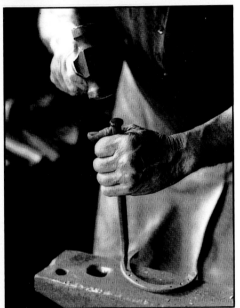

Above: Gordon W. Richards' string with JonJo O'Neill in the foreground utilise natural facilities during training

Left: Blacksmith Vic Alderton who shod *Battleship* to win the 1938 Grand National outside his Eastbury forge seen still making his own horseshoes

Below: Roger Charlton exercises a horse in his equine pool

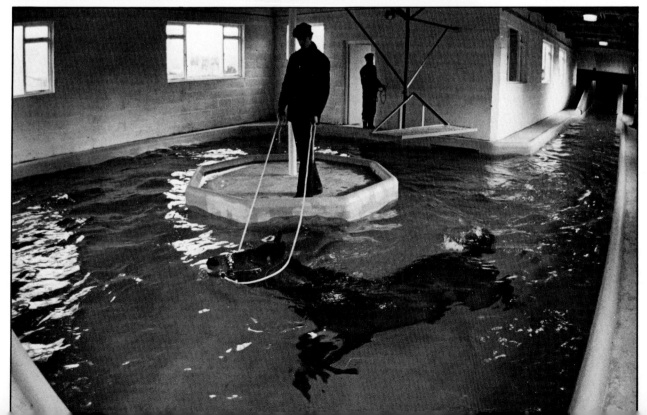

Fred Winter and his head lad Brian Delaney stride to start
an early morning schooling session

They are not all willing!

Brian Delaney and assistant
trainer the Hon. Stephen
Stanhope equip *Elmaco*
with blinkers to
improve his
concentration

A seasoned performer leads youngster with Lord Oaksey
up, over hurdles

One of Josh Gifford's young horses leaps carefully
between two of his elders at Findon

Two novice chasers are led over the fences by a
schoolmaster watched by the trainer Fred Winter

Fulke Walwyn — Lambourn

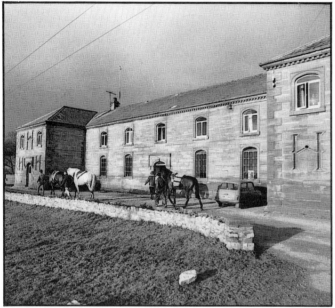
Gordon W. Richards — Penrith

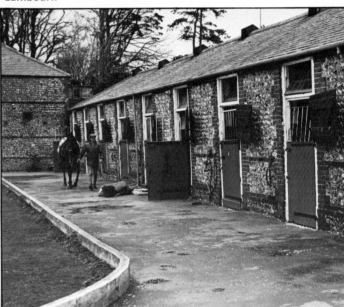
Josh Gifford — Findon

Jim Dreaper — County Dublin

Fred Winter — Lambourn

118

A good man with no facilities will do a better job than a moderate one with all the aids.

The ideal length of time that a horse needs to stay at a livery yard for breaking in will depend upon the time and money available. The longer that it can stay at a breakers yard the better in the long run, because undoubtedly there will be more time to devote to the youngster's education. It is a natural assumption to the layman that horses are born obedient to man, but nothing is further from the truth. Stage by stage, through repetition and reward a horse's wild instincts are curbed until it is obedient to its masters. If, as sometimes is necessary, there has to be a battle then the handler must win or else be prepared to face double the trouble the following day. In cases where time is limited to three days for the complete process a purgative is given to the animal to weaken its defences. The end product is a horse that can be ridden but one that is definitely not broken in. When there is no time limit through lack of labour or money a normal horse will be broken and educated in six weeks. Having persuaded the animal to accept the first stage of a horse's training, the breaking in, then the task of getting it fit and schooled to jump racing obstacles is the next stage.

In my view there are many smaller trainers who for a variety of reasons rarely make the news but can, and do, get the very best possible results from the limited material at their disposal. The way in which most trainers ply their trade varies tremendously, even amongst the largest and longest standing of them. Most of the methods seem to eventually arrive at the right result. The basics, which are the common denominators, are most important. These are proper feeding and general good health. It is when the actual galloping comes into play that the individual methods become evident.

Trainers, especially when they enter the big time, need to delegate. There are just not enough hours in the day for one man to attend to all the necessary jobs. The first and most important person that a trainer will employ is the head man. He will need to be a person who will do the trainer's bidding equally as well when he is away racing or at home with his eye on the job. A head man's job is not an easy one. He will need to be an expert feeder, be prepared to turn out at 6 a.m. thirteen days out of fourteen, have a constant eye for the tell-tale symptoms that herald any one of a thousand ailments, and also to be able to manage a staff.

The feeding of a racehorse is a delicate operation. As they become fitter they tend to live on their nerves not wanting to eat enough of the high-quality concentrate foods that are deemed necessary to maintain their energy bank. To persuade a highly strung racehorse to eat a sufficiently balanced diet is not exactly easy, sometimes it is almost impossible. Indeed as they get fitter they will often sort out the ingredients that they do not like in their feed, eating the rest, or what they consider to be the best, and leaving that which they do not like in the bottom of the manger. In order to tempt a horse to eat, all sorts of sweeteners are added to feeds, including chopped carrots, grass, molasses or sugar-beet pulp.

There are many additives marketed now by various feed firms, all of whom immediately claim credit when a horse wins a big race. But let us not forget that horses were winning big races when there were just good oats, chaff and bran to feed upon, their winning times still holding good today. *Red Rum* and *Crisp* broke the Grand National record time that had stood for 40 years when they fought for the 1973 honours. Here again trainers swear by their own methods of feeding. Some like to use Scotch oats, whilst a large number have turned to Australian oats which are far more expensive but in return, uniformity can be guaranteed for an entire season because of the large quantity that dealers have to import at one time. A certain number of them will advocate a mixed diet of oats and horse nuts. The nuts are produced by the big milling firms to combine all the necessary protein, carbohydrates, vitamins and roughage that the equine athletes need to keep them at peak fitness. In fact they are so complete that no hay need be fed to animals whose diet consists solely of this concentrate. However, the majority of trainers who do not feed solely nuts believe that the hours a horse spends eating hay performs the all important task of occupying a racehorse's time as well as providing the required roughage during the $22\frac{1}{2}$ hours that he will spend in his stable each day. Even so there are winning trainers who do feed nuts without hay, so it is difficult to say who is right.

The stable staff also come under the head man's jurisdiction in order to leave the trainer free to do the entries for races, look through the many sales catalogues, sort out the race presenting the best chance of winning, and to spend hours on the telephone. The importance of a good head man cannot be underlined enough, having started at 6 a.m. he will spend an hour going around the horses giving them a bowl of oats for their breakfast, observing them in complete peace and quiet. This helps form in his mind an accurate picture of their general condition. Whilst going from box to box, the head man will only feed each horse providing it has finished the previous evening's feed. If he has not done so the stale food will be removed before any fresh food is added to the manger. He will observe the horse's general condition and the state of the stable to see if the droppings were either too wet, too hard or non-existent. He will look at the horse's eyes, generally taking in points to enable him to give an accurate

Overleaf:
Gordon Richards' string seen exercising on a winter's morning at Greystoke, near Penrith

Fred and Mercy Rimell

Peter Easterby

Fulke Walwyn

precis of all the inmates' condition to the trainer when he first sees him. All this must be done in the space of thirty seconds per box in order to complete the rounds before the other staff arrive.

In a stable which houses a fair number of horses, there are certain to be a percentage with leg trouble. The head man will inspect all the troublesome legs at this same time every morning, reporting their condition to the trainer and advising any necessary steps which should be taken. The trainer will listen to his head man, although he has the last word of course. This hour spent when all is quiet is then relayed to the trainer in the space of five minutes; '*Blackie* is worried about something, he's walked his box all night.' 'I don't like the look of that new Irish horse, his eye is pink, and his coat is starey.' 'The three we ran yesterday all ate up, I've left the bandages on until after breakfast.' 'The big fellow's legs are fine, but I would like you to look at the white-faced horse in the corner box.' The trainer and the head man will then sort out the various problems whilst the lads muck-out the stables and tack up the first lot of horses to be exercised. Most stables will have some sort of list drawn up indicating who rides what, with the larger concerns boasting magnetic boards displaying at a moment's glance the inmates and the available riders.

The most common trainers' disease is 'irritability', which is undoubtedly generated by the amount of pressure that comes to bear when a man is training horses owned by other people. The one thing that most often starts the shouting is pure frustration caused by things not going to plan. Most of the top trainers have been riders at some stage so when, having carefully explained the proposed gallops, lads either do not or cannot carry them out it is only natural for the trainer to think 'Things ain't what they used to be.' The utter helplessness of the trainer when lads flash past him at the wrong speeds is usually converted to verbal abuse which more often than not is carried away on the wind. Certain trainers realising that they are not the best judge of a young horse leave the selecting and buying of new stock to a Bloodstock Agent, although they undoubtedly will have expressed a firm opinion as to their likes and dislikes.

The importance of buying the right animal cannot be stressed enough. That is why most trainers employ 'eyes' to seek out well bred youngsters with good conformation, or in the case of horses with form, those with potential to train on. To spend years educating and bringing a horse to peak fitness is nothing but a waste of time and money if the animal is wrong from the start. During a horse's National Hunt racing career many things are liable to give a trainer further worry, but none more than unsoundness in the legs or wind, or possibly both! These ailments afflict a high percentage of the jumpers in training, the cause is bad parentage, bad conformation or bad handling either from the rider or the trainer. For every bargain you read about, rest assured there will have been thousands of similarly priced horses which turn out to be expensive. It costs more to train a useless racehorse than a good one, because the former will not contribute towards his keep, whereas the good one, may, even after statutory 'presents' (ie 10 per cent to the jockey and trainer and $4\frac{1}{2}$ per cent to the stable lads) have been deducted, pay his way.

Let us assume that a well formed youngster has been properly broken in and is ready to go on to serious training. He will be given to one of the stable staff to care for during his time in that stable. The horse's lad/lass will attend to the horse's well being and cleanliness throughout the day along with possibly two other horses. In most cases they will also exercise their charges on six days a week, thus establishing a strong bond between them. Because jumpers are eligible to start 'timber topping' (jumping hurdles as opposed to fences) in the autumn of their third year, often continuing until they are 13 years old, their handlers come to regard them as their property, purely lending the horses to their owners just for the racing days. This love and devotion is rewarded by a wage of approximately £50 a week, and despite the hard work on the part of the staff by the TWGU in conjunction with The Stable Lads Association, not all of them are receiving that amount yet.

For the first few days in training the horse will be exercised gently and not fed to its maximum in order to size up its attributes or bad habits despite probably having received a brief from the previous handler. It also gives the horse a chance to settle into its new surroundings.

According to a horse's make, shape and character or in the case of a known performer his form, a trainer will map out a training campaign. All horses need time spent walking and trotting around roads to turn some of their fat into muscle, or in the case of animals in poor condition to put muscle where formerly there was none. Over-gross animals may look fine to their proud owners, but often they need half a season to get fit enough to be safe to work seriously.

Once the trainer has categorised an animal he will exercise it accordingly. Most horses' programmes will have the same content, it will be the amount that differs. A normal jumper will require up to eight weeks brisk walking and trotting before cantering exercise starts. Usually this type of work will take an hour and a half on the roads, preferably to include hills of up to 1 in 8 gradients. This stage can become both boring and uncomfortable, but nevertheless it is a very important part of the build-up process. It is boring for the rider who knows the daily route back to front, and having once taken advantage of his lofty position on the animal's back by looking into hitherto private places, he loses interest. The horse also tires of the daily

123

Jim Dreaper's string at Kilsallaghan near Dublin

trotting, the idle ones become increasingly hard to keep going whilst the sharp characters, feeling the benefit of their new-found fitness, need only the slightest excuse to misbehave. A certain amount of discomfort usually arises due to both horse and rider hardening to work after a summer away from the saddle. The equines usually suffer from sore backs and girths, whilst their human partners are constantly reminded of their chafed areas each time they bump the saddle at the trot!

As the training progresses the horse's food intake is increased to approximately 18 lb a day, though there are people who claim to feed up to 24 lb a day. All I can say to that is that maybe they do manage to attain that poundage for a short period but to maintain it throughout the season when the animal is in regular work or racing would be a rare occurrence. A 'good doer', ie a horse who eats everything he is given, is a boon in a racing yard; a horse will stand any amount of work if it eats its feeds, and conversely will have to be treated tenderly if a shy feeder.

Up to this point trainers will not have differed very much in their methods, it is when the cantering or galloping starts that they vary. Once the horses are hardened enough to begin cantering, a new excitement is aroused amongst the staff, probably the same as the day the animals entered the yard at the start of the

season. They will probably canter for one and a half miles on two days in the first week, gradually increasing the work mornings to four occasions per week in the third week. A general pattern then emerges; road work on Mondays, cantering on Tuesday, fast work on Wednesday followed by a hot bran mash for the evening feed, a quiet walk around the village for half-an-hour on Thursday, canter on Friday, fast work on Saturday again followed by a mash feed, and finally either a lead out to pick grass or even a rest day in the stable on Sunday. This is only a general pattern of work.

The places that are used to exercise horses and the methods employed when carrying out the work vary from the sublime to the ridiculous. All produce winners which bears out the supposition that good feeding and general health are the important factors governing success. Without doubt, having attained a fair level of fitness, the next step is to keep the animal mentally happy. Although horses are clothed, fed and groomed in addition to having their stables cleaned twice daily, they are in solitary confinement for, at the least, 21 hours out of every 24.

It is interesting to see exactly how much interest a horse does take in the general comings and goings in a stableyard when weather conditions permit the top half of the stable doors to be left open. This factor is

Fulke Walwyn's string returning to stables from Lambourn Downs

even more important with jumpers than flat racehorses because they may spend ten or more years in the same surroundings. It is notable that horses which lose their form usually return to the winners' enclosure following a change of trainer. It does not follow that the second trainer is any better than the first, the rejuvenating factor is the complete change in surroundings. This applies to the horses that leave their best racecourse form ominously behind them, not the majority of horses in training who give their best every time they race. The grand old, almost black gelding *Sonny Sommers* has retained his form even in his seventeenth year, having spent twelve years in the same stable.

The simplest method of keeping horses happy is to try to use as many different routes and gallops as possible each week. Also turning horses out into a small paddock for an hour after each morning's exercise is a proven remedy for stale or worried racers. Only certain horses react to this treatment, although some tend to stand moping in one place feeling sorry for themselves. A small paddock is best suited for this purpose so that the animals do not gallop around running risk of injury which in steeplechasing happens easily enough anyway. If a horse does respond to this form of therapy, it can be done safely even in cold weather by the addition of a waterproof rug which will keep it both dry and warm. The Irish trainers do this on

a far greater scale than their English counterparts, even to the extent of turning 15 or more fully shod, fit horses into one paddock after exercise. But then the Irishmen generally train their horses as close to nature as possible.

Water is also therapeutic in keeping a horse sound in mind and limb. Often horses are swum to maintain their fitness when suffering from leg trouble which would not allow them to be galloped, but also swimming is used as a change of work for moody characters. There have been a lot of equine pools built in recent years to cater for the need, one of which operates in Lambourn. It was built by Roger Charlton in 1974 at Windsor House Stables, the yard in which Peter Walwyn started his memorable career. It has now been passed on to new trainer Nicky Henderson who will operate it on a separate basis to his training yard, in order to satisfy the ruling authorities. It is, however, not necessary to have such a lavish place to swim horses in. Nicky's father-in-law, the intrepid 52-year-old amateur jockey, permit holder and stud owner John Thorne, has made his own by digging a 30 ft deep trench, 10 ft wide, which is fed by a diverted stream, thus ensuring fresh water at all times. Though not the first to use the sea, probably the most publicised trainer is Ginger McCain who proved the value of saline water as a preventative, if not cure, for

Pat Taaffe's horses at
exercise, relaxing
afterwards, and (below)
the trainer on board
Captain Christy

Trainer Jim Dreaper takes *Ten Up* to a stream, whilst canine help is enlisted at his Kilsallaghan, County Dublin stables and the secret recipe is cooked for the twice weekly mash

Early morning schooling for Gordon Richards' horse at Greystoke

pedal osteitis which is inflammation of the pedal bone. Even in the 1977/78 season when his main stay *Red Rum* retired, Ginger established numerically his best season despite having to work with middling performers. Other trainers who use natural waterways are Penrith trainer Gordon Richards and Irish trainer Jim Dreaper.

The facilities for galloping jumpers are important but not as crucial as those needed for the flat racehorses, and contrary to popular belief it is not necessary to gallop horses over the distance that they race over. If a horse is in good health and well prepared from its roadwork it just needs to be 'topped up' once a week by strong work and kept supple on three other days by one and a quarter mile canters or half speeds. 'Stuffy' horses will obviously need to be galloped more often to keep their wind pipes clear, whilst slightly built or excitable horses can often be kept straight on the lunge rein. So basically once a horse is fit it is a case of common sense to keep it simmering and bringing it to the boil on race days.

The 600 acres of communal gallops in Lambourn provide every facility needed to bring to, and keep jumpers at, peak fitness whilst Tony Dickinson who has constantly produced the highest rate of winners to runners from his Gisburn (Lancashire) stables has to

transport his horses elsewhere whenever they require a gallop. Most, but not all jumping trainers advocate very little real galloping, they like horses to quicken readily, but always 'on the bridle', ie with the riders still keeping a hold of the horse's head, not pushing it along with a loose rein. Home trials amongst steeplechasers are a rare occurrence because of the large part the jumping element has to play in the end result. If punters watched a string of jumpers work for a month, it is my guess that they would back far more losers than they had ever done before! The dual Champion Hurdler, *Bula*, never sparked at home except on schooling mornings when the obstacles transformed him into a 'machine'.

Obviously proper schooling constitutes a fair percentage of a successful horse's training. If the animal is introduced to small jumps when being broken in it is a real advantage, but only in terms of the length of time it takes to get an animal to the racing stage. Basically the golden rule regarding jumping is the same when teaching any horse to jump, whether it be hurdles, fences, show jumping or hunting. Before attempting to leave the ground, a horse must be as obedient as possible to its rider's commands, it must also have done a lot of ground work in order to be balanced and co-ordinated. Then at a trot or slow canter they continue to clear it with precision and confidence. Speed leads to jumping from desperation, ending in either a confused or frightened animal. In Paul Kelleway's words, 'Any fool can get a horse buzzing, it takes a horseman to switch one off.' When, and only when, a horse knows how he got from one side of the obstacle to the other and does so with complete composure should he face bigger obstacles at a faster pace. Far more ground and energy are lost by an animal that gallops straight on with complete disregard for an obstacle than one which jumps with precision, albeit a little slower. Many trainers have small solid jumps to make the pupil respect their task, for a horse that takes liberties with its jump will undoubtedly pay the penalty sooner or later resulting at best in the loss of a race and at worst loss of life.

Loose schooling is also widely used — Fred Rimell being its greatest disciple. His loose school is enclosed but not covered, is oval in shape and has two fixed but adjustable jumps, one each along the 50 ft long sides. He stands in the middle of the school cracking a hunting crop when he sees that the riderless horse is on the right stride for take-off. The value of loose schooling is that a horse gets into and consequently gets out of its own trouble. Once they understand that there is a way around they continue to jump for fun, many having to be forcibly stopped by the trainer standing in the way. In fact Fred Rimell ran and won over hurdles with *Normandy* (winner of Irish Sweeps Hurdle and now at stud) straight from the loose school. Another advantage of the loose school is that as many as forty obstacles can be negotiated as opposed to only six by a ridden horse in a similar time on a conventional schooling ground. One thing is for certain, it is advisable to finish on a good note. Sending a horse to jump again after a good display, purely for the fun, can be disastrous or at best upset the previous good work.

A trainer's biggest and ever-present worry is injury to, or infirmity in, his charges. As clever as the master is at spotting the first signs of trouble, he would be foolish not to listen to his head man and the lad who looks after the horse, should they think all is not well. Disappointing as it may be for all concerned when the warning signs present themselves shortly before a race, it is less costly in time and money to heed them rather than to take the risk of ignoring them, desperately hoping they will disappear.

However, even though the man-hours spent training jumpers and the burden of 24 hours a day worry makes the job appear unattractive, there are more people than ever willing to risk their capital in this risky, but satisfying profession!

Dawn breaks on a winter's morning at Josh Gifford's yard at Findon

Early morning gallops by Gordon W. Richards' horses

Breakfast is snatched by the staff, between first and
second lots, in the tack room

A dull start to the day

Night Nurse and *Easby Abbey* utilise the straw barn for exercise in frozen conditions

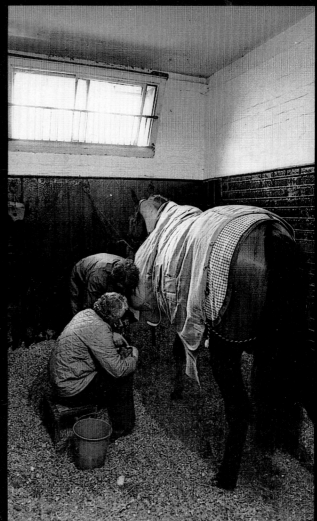

Comedy of Errors leads home Fred Rimell's string at Kinnersley near Worcester

Auriol Sinclair inspects a horse's foot during her evening

One of the daily chores — changing the bedding at Peter Easterby's stable

Good stablemen are hard to find — two of Stan Mellor's staff

Jack Kidd, 25 years travelling head man for Fred Rimell, trains the yard cat to jump as expertly as the horses

'Friends'

8 Jumping, the object of the exercise

You cannot win if you do not complete the course. This obvious statement is a basic rule that trainers drum into aspiring jockeys, though all too often they return with grass stains on their white breeches to tell their mount's connections 'We were only in third gear at the time, all the rest were struggling; we would have won by a mile if we had not fallen at the second last fence.' Racewatchers on occasions will mutter about so-and-so sitting too still at the obstacles — 'Probably his nerve has gone.' More than likely he has learned the error of 'asking' a horse to continually stand off a long way from his obstacles. Experience in steeplechases has to be earned the hard way, quite often at a very high price.

The object of the exercise is to negotiate the fences or hurdles with speed and accuracy using as little energy as possible in the process. Flamboyant leaps look impressive from the grandstand and feel fantastic from the saddle, but if asked for purely for those reasons can be disastrous. There are times in every race, when for a multitude of reasons 'a long one' is needed to get a combination out of trouble, or less often to get someone else into trouble. A young jockey riding with youthful exuberance may ask the maximum from his partner at the obstacles more often than a seasoned jockey who has learned the cost of his uncalled for bravado, but that does not mean the old rider is any less brave.

A jockey needs to get himself out of trouble in the majority of his races, whereas he will only try to get a fellow rider into difficulties on odd occasions. There is practically no foul play these days, though a certain amount of gamesmanship is recognised and accepted. There will be times when a race has roughly formed its eventual pattern when a rider, knowing that his mount will respond to any question asked of him, will attempt to rush upside an opponent on the approach to a fence kicking for take-off a stride earlier than is normal in the hope that his opponent's horse subconsciously rises at the same time but without the required impulsion. The result is doubly beneficial to the former, for not only does he gain valuable ground but his opponent has been surprised into a projection which costs him both distance and, more important, energy.

It is this sort of use of a rider's guile and his horse's obedience that the bulk of the racing public do not see, or if they do they probably do not always interpret. That is why it is a good idea to occasionally walk down the track in order to 'read' a race as it really is, and that does not mean just to the last fence. You may have to turn a blind eye to some of the language used, or even be prepared to accept the resultant emotions from a fall. One thing can be guaranteed — there is far more to jumping than can ever be envisaged by grandstand spectators. For instance there is a time when, even though momentarily, the tumultuous noise made by the field as it sweeps towards a fence ceases. It is of course the moment of lift-off when pounding hooves become airborne. The silence is, however, short lived. Horses either brush through the top of a fence, landing safely on the far side, most of them grunting as they do so, or get too close to the fence, inevitably crashing through it.

The times in a race when riders 'ask for a long one' to extricate themselves from trouble or simply to gain ground, are both frequent and noticeable. However, that is only one way of securing a clear round, the second is to 'take a pull', to shorten a horse's stride, which as I have already said punters often interpret as loss of nerve. The decision to 'ask' or 'pull' is obvious to a seasoned jockey as experience has taught him to weigh up every situation on its merits, whereas youngsters nearly always opt for the former. That is fine providing the equine partner has the necessary scope and trust in his rider to answer the request, but as the race progresses, steadily taking its toll on energy resources, the awful moment of truth comes when the mind is still willing but the flesh is weak! When this happens the message of the impending crash flashes to the brain which in turn stimulates the survival procedure. In the split second before impact, an established jockey grips with his knees, bracing himself for the inevitable shock as half a ton of horse flesh travelling at upwards of thirty miles an hour comes to a sudden halt. However, the weight and speed of the horse ensures that the partnership is stationary for only a split second before pursuing its course, albeit different from the intended one. Any rider not sure of the meaning of momentum, having been involved in the aforementioned incident, will no longer be in doubt.

133

Who says horses don't jump?

Night Nurse and Paddy Broderick go for a long one

First jump at Cheltenham Gold Cup 1972. No. 5, Terry
Biddlecombe on *Gay Trip*

Procedure before a race — showing a horse what he has to jump

It never ceases to amaze me how often horses survive serious mistakes even if the rider does not manage to keep the partnership intact. Having blundered badly, becoming riderless in the process, the majority of horses do continue in the race, more often than not jumping faultlessly, which makes one wonder if a lot of the mistakes a horse makes are man-made. Occasionally riderless horses do fall and this is a fact which is immediately noted by the jockeys who quickly spread the word amongst their colleagues, resulting in a hard time for the trainer the next time it races should he require a 'spare' jockey.

Although obstacles do vary from venue to venue they are basically the same. The rules of racing require fences to be no lower than 4 ft 6 in except for the water jump, but fence builders throughout the country hold widely differing views as to the desirable solidity of the fence. This, combined with the varying gradients of racecourses, gives horses far from uniformity in the obstacles they are asked to jump. It is laid down by the rules of racing that in the first two miles of a steeplechase there must be at least twelve fences, with no less than six more in each succeeding mile. The four and a half mile Grand National, for instance, has thirty fences.

It is a good thing that fences do vary in severity because if the Aintree fences, or for that matter those at Cheltenham or Newbury, were transferred *en masse* to Plumpton or Cartmel there would undoubtedly be a serious drain on The Injured Jockeys Fund! Some years ago the Plumpton fences were remade to a much stiffer standard than their predecessors, resulting in

Worm's eye view as the field hit a hurdle and knock it to the ground

S. Jobar takes the Open Ditch at Kempton Park in the Portwine Novice Steeplechase

Pendil leads *Game Spirit* over the water jump at Newbury

No. 9, Macer Gifford on *Speonk* and Tommy Stack on *Cerulean* fighting it out over the last hurdle at Windsor

Left: All systems go! *Top left to right:* Lord Oaksey, John Francome.
Bottom left to right: Richard Pitman, Stan Mellor

Above left: Andy Turnell is forced to sit behind the saddle, due to his unique short style of riding, when his mount takes a long leap

Above right: Bill Smith and *Fort Devon*, a former winner of the Maryland Hunt Cup in the USA, show their paces at Kempton Park

Having exceeded the jump over Becher's Brook, horse and jockey try to maintain their balance

serious representations by the riders to the local stewards who were not at first unduly concerned. The men whose livelihoods depended on staying intact, decided a practical demonstration was called for, so led by the flamboyant Barry Brogan they walked in line along the top of the tightly packed birch providing good press photographs as well as proving their point. Thankfully the Plumpton executive modified them before the next race meeting.

It is foolish to assume that horses only fall at stiff fences; any fence no matter how soft can alter the result of a race. To jump around a course successfully the combination needs to be in unison with the rider giving the instructions and his mount obeying them. Jockeys are bracketed in three ways; they are considered to be horsemen, jockeys or plain cowboys. Many take offence at being labelled as horsemen, though to my mind it is a great compliment. Simple mathematics tell us that the man who presents his horse at the fences in such a fashion that he meets them on a normal stride, with no extra exertion needed to ensure a clean leap, will undoubtedly save many lengths in the process. During a three mile chase with eighteen jumps to negotiate, a horseman could save a conservative average of half a length per jump, giving him a nine length advantage on a rival considered to be a superior jockey. Having gained that amount of ground throughout the race the jockey would need to be a real hindrance to lose this same amount of ground on the run from the last fence to the winning post. Ideally riders should be a combination of both a horseman and a jockey, as indeed most of them are. Two modern-day riders stand out head and shoulders above the rest as horsemen, namely John Francome and Michael Dickinson. Sadly Michael was forced to retire from the saddle in August 1978 due to his injury. They can and do get horses to jump without any visible aids, and as a consequence are a joy to watch. Close behind them come Ron Barry and Bob Champion, whilst in the 'all jockey' group, JonJo O'Neill is the king pin. Graham Thorner, David Goulding and Andy Turnell figure high in this league, with Bob Davies, the now retired Tommy Stack, Richard Linley and Colin Tinkler leading the field in the combined jockey/horseman group. In retrospect any race narrowly lost, should have been won 'If only he had gone around the inside', 'What would have happened had he kicked at the ditch', 'At least three lengths were lost when he missed the second last', 'If that horse ever learns to jump water he will take some beating.' But jumping is the name of the game, and hopefully always will be because once the element of chance is eliminated the sport will lose its appeal.

Left: Bill Smith has an uncomfortable moment but retains his seat on *Exhibit B* at Newbury

The exact advantage gained by quick, clean, economical jumping cannot be measured with a great deal of certainty. If, for example, you watch two horses jump down the railway straight at Sandown, which provides seven fences in a straight line with the last three less than one hundred yards apart, it is easy for even the untrained eye to calculate the exact advantage one horse has gained over the other.

However, the lengths gained may have been costly in terms of the energy used if the horse had been employing over-extravagant leaps. One thing is certain though, the ground gained in the air is far less expensive than the lengths gained by galloping, providing the jumping is accurate rather than desperate which does undoubtedly have a taxing result. The ideal compromise is for a horse to meet each fence in his normal stride, neither checking nor extending in order to jump it cleanly. This of course rarely, if ever, happens for the whole duration of a race, though without doubt horses ridden by Michael Dickinson and John Francome have far more flawless rounds than those ridden by any other present-day rider.

A horse can be said to 'meet' a fence correctly when he takes-off to jump it at a point about twice as far away from the ground line as the height of the fence itself. This combined with the fact that most fences are sloped from the take-off board to the top of the fence, forming a spread of six feet, gives a horse roughly thirteen feet in which to gain the necessary height to clear it. As the top of the fence has been tapered down to only eighteen inches or less, it is hardly surprising that a half ton horse travelling at thirty miles an hour can brush through the top six inches without seriously endangering his chances of making a safe landing.

Ideally speaking a horse should touch down an equal distance from the fence as from where he took-off, and having done so, without any undue hindrance should be into his stride and away without a break. If the approach has for any one of many reasons been checked the horse will put in 'a short stride' going almost up to the take-off board before rising. In doing so he will have to jump much higher in order to clear the fence, and consequently his trajectory will have been much more severe than the first described jump. He will, as a result, land steeply, maybe even in a heap having covered only twelve feet as opposed to the proper jump of double that distance. In addition to the ground lost the impetus is less and much more energy is needed to regain the normal gallop. Another energy sapping situation is when a horse stands off from a fence without his jockey's instruction two strides before the ideal spot. When this happens the moment of realisation that the combination is landing before the fence has actually been cleared is not one to be recommended, nor included in a rider's 'moments to be treasured'. Occasionally a horse in this position,

A bad mistake due to the combination standing off too far

A mistake sends a shower of leaves from a newly-constructed fence at the start of a season

Left: A view only seen by fallen jockeys

All clear at the water jump

Reflection in the Fontwell Park Water Jump — the widest obstacle in a steeplechase

The field taking The Chair during the 1977 Grand National showing its width as well as its much publicised height

Fish-eye lens technique capturing the landing during a steeplechase

Tommy Stack and Jane Thorne fight out the 1978
Whitbread Gold Cup Steeplechase two jumps from home

realising his plight, stretches in mid air in an effort to
avoid the impending collision, but this is indeed the
exception, not the rule. *Tingle Creek* and *Pendil* were
two horses with such ability, and as a result
commanded a huge public following.

Ground conditions have a considerable bearing on
the length of a horse's stride, and consequently his style
of jumping. During the wet months which make up a
good half of the National Hunt season, and
particularly when the bulk of the major races are
decided, a horse has a much shorter stride, lending
itself to less flamboyant leaps than those obtained on
fast or good going. Undoubtedly the better the
partnership the further away from an obstacle they can
weigh it up, making the necessary adjustment of stride.
Both Dickinson and Francome seem to either meet
fences on the correct stride, or to go for a lengthened
stride, the latter only when necessary to avoid trouble.
This is of course no coincidence. It is a result of eyeing
the jump from afar, and making the required adjustment whilst some of their fellow riders are thinking
purely of their style, or other less important subjects.
In order to do this a clear view of a fence is required,
which in large fields, especially early in the race, is
not always possible. A successful rider must be able,
having selected his path and suddenly finding his way
blocked by a loose horse or unreliable colleagues, to

change his course at a split second's notice; and what's
more his decision must be right.

There are horses which jump well only when
completely blinded at a fence. These horses are
generally faint-hearted, but as jumping is a natural
part of a horse's make-up, instinct comes into play and
they rise when the horse immediately preceding them
picks up. This means that they have taken off a stride
early which gives spectators the impression that the
animal is a brave jumper, but in fact this is far from the
truth. The same horse if shown a lot of 'daylight' would
drop his bridle, decreasing his speed with each stride.
Having lost ground on his rivals in the process, he
would finally almost climb the fence. Being faced with
this sort of ride is not a pleasant situation because
although they know they can 'play a tune' on their
unwilling partner by forcing his head in behind
another horse's tail, survival depends largely on the
lead horse's own ability to negotiate the obstacles
successfully. The feeling, having committed oneself in
this fashion, when the lead horse either hits a fence or
stumbles on landing, makes the £20 fee seem far from
lucrative. Happily such animals are in the minority.

Conversely there are also horses who, when catching
sight of a fence quicken rapidly of their own accord
paying little or no heed to their jockey. In such cases a
rider is best advised to sit still, take a firm grip of the
horse's head without actually pulling him out of his
stride, and prepare for 'a stand off' or 'fiddle' when the
obstacle is reached. In this case because the horse is

Tightly packed field in the George Duller Handicap Hurdle race at the Cheltenham Festival Meeting 1972

Neck and neck in the Jacky Upton Opportunity Steeplechase at Newbury for young riders

Not too much room to spare when taking a hurdle at speed

The chips are down as *Monksfield*, *Dramatist* and *Night Nurse* fight it out over the last hurdle

A well contested amateur chase at the March Meeting at Cheltenham

At this fence Jeff King, No. 9, goes to the buckle end of the reins whilst Bob Davies sits up the neck and Michael Dickinson looks for some daylight

Top right: The Field taking Becher's Brook in the Topham Steeplechase, Liverpool 1972

Lower right: Tapes start at Folkestone

Above: A fine leap in the lead by The Queen Mother's *Inch Arran* ridden by Richard Dennard

Below left: Worried looks from the spectators as Jeff King's mount jumps too high at the water jump

Below: Full stretch over the ditch

Proud Tarquin and Paul Kelleway get too close before take off. They stumble forfeiting a length and the race to the Ron Smythe trained *New Romney*

increasing his speed rapidly on the approach to the jump, it is impossible to gauge the exact position of lift-off until it is actually reached. Horses who have a habit of racing in this fashion invariably jump well unless hindered by their jockey. *Crisp* opened up such a commanding lead in the record breaking 1973 Grand National for this very reason. As he landed over each obstacle his stride could be checked but only until he caught sight of the following fence. He would then race at it as if he wanted to devour it. To interfere with such a horse would be foolish and belittling.

The horse who broke the record in 1973, *Red Rum*, went on to become an Aintree legend, attracting a serious bid of £500000 from a Japanese impresario who could see the enormous entertainment potential that went hand in glove with such exploits. If we examine the reasons why *Red Rum* was three times the winner and twice second in the Grand National from his only five starts, it becomes patently obvious that his style of jumping lent itself to the saving of vital energy, which in turn enabled his strength to last out when most other horses' lungs and muscles were crying 'enough'. Each year at Aintree *Red Rum* could keep in contention by jumping his fences economically, neither standing off too far, nor getting too close to the base. Television cameras showed the world how he pricked his ears thirty yards before each fence, obviously weighing it up, seeing his own stride, and if necessary doing an 'Ali shuffle' to change his leading leg in order to meet the obstacle correctly. In the five years that he thrilled us over the Aintree fences I can only remember him making one mistake when pecking on landing at the fourth last in the 1974 race when ridden by Brian

Fletcher who was his partner on three occasions, winning on two of them. This means that he negotiated one hundred and fifty obstacles there, taking drops, turns, ditches to and away, spreads and catchy plain fences all in his stride. Truly an amazing performance, especially from a horse bred to win sprints on the flat.

All riders are faced with the same problem, the task only differing with the size and speed at which an obstacle has to be jumped, to find an answer to the question 'Where is the last stride going to land me?' A jockey does not need to be nearly so precise as a show jumper for instance, but he does have to contend with far more variables and dangers. However, the basic question is just the same, and the answer will still be one of these three; 'too close', 'too far away', or 'spot on!'

A good jump by Ron Barry and *The Dikler* puts him in contention as Bobby Beasley and *Captain Christy* make a mistake at the last fence in the 1974 Cheltenham Gold Cup only to recover and win

Uncle Bing and John Francome match flight with a swan in the King George VI Chase on Boxing Day

Take-off at the rear of Hurdle race at Windsor

After a race at Plumpton on a winter's day

9 Falls

There is no such thing as a good fall, it is simply that some hurt less than others. Even if horse and jockey rise after a crash with no physical pain on either side, the horse will be suffering from uncertainty and his partner from dented pride.

For some reason a rider fails to complete the course on 10 per cent of the times he starts out, which numerically for a regular jockey means 'hitting the deck' on approximately forty five occasions per season. Of those, thirty five will be painful without being serious enough to stop him riding again that same day, even though all his moving parts may not be functioning to the same degree as when the day's sport began. Of the other ten falls nine will be severe beatings and one will be a show stopper! If a rider gets away with the last named he would not want to bet heavily that he could repeat the feat twice in succession. Broken collar bones, sprung ribs, dislocated backs, wrists or ankles are commonplace, which with specialist treatment and expert strapping necessitate only minor periods of incapacity. For eighteen months now concussion has been treated seriously with statutory periods of convalescence ranging from one to three weeks according to the severity of the bout. At first this ruling did not go down at all well with the riders of fancied horses in big races when forced to miss the opportunity of glory and a decent pay cheque. Coincidentally both the 1977 and 1978 Champion Hurdles were the two main races affected in this way and ironically neither resulted in a lost victory. In 1977 Andy Turnell suffered concussion on the first day of the Festival Meeting forfeiting the ride on *Birds Nest* who attracted as much monetary support as the drops of rain that fell in the interim. Steve Knight replaced Andy after several abortive representations on the latter's behalf. *Birds Nest* never really looked like winning although Andy, having recovered from his initial disappointment, would have been delighted had *Birds Nest* stormed up the finishing hill to take the hurdling crown. History repeated itself a year later when following a month of 'will he — won't he' JonJo O'Neill opted to ride *Sea Pigeon* in preference to the dual champion *Night Nurse*. Fate intervened when *Grangewood Girl* fell on the first day of the meeting to leave the champion elect unconscious on the turf.

Though a bitter blow to *Sea Pigeon*'s connections it was a great relief to know that all JonJo had lost was a week's riding. Within half an hour *Night Nurse*'s intended rider Colin Tinkler suffered a crashing fall at the downhill fence which during two days ended so many Irish dreams of collecting bundles of unearned income. Colin rose from the grass limping badly towards the safety of the running rails, then in true professional fashion remembering his engagement with *Night Nurse* and realising his trainer was undoubtedly weighing up the situation through his binoculars, he forced himself to walk soundly, in fact almost defiantly, to the Doctor's Land Rover. It was at first thought that Colin had broken a bone in his foot, so imagine trainer Peter Easterby's plight at having to find suitable replacement jockeys for both the first and second favourites for the hurdling crown just twenty four hours before the race.

One senior rider who already had a mount in the race said every jockey not booked to ride in it immediately came up with a good reason why he should be the chosen one. 'They sought out Peter Easterby with their claims, swamping him as if he was about to give £2000 away instead of the chance of earning it.' The Irish jockey Frank Berry was chosen to partner *Sea Pigeon* and 'Big' Ron Barry for *Night Nurse*, though in the end Colin Tinkler was fit enough to ride the latter after passing the Doctor's examination on the day of the race. *Sea Pigeon* threw down his challenge on the run to the final hurdle, needing a good jump to put him level with *Monksfield*. Although he did not make a mistake he got slightly too close to the obstacle to obtain an advantage and was held at bay by the deserved winner right to the winning post. Whilst this was happening JonJo was verbally urging *Sea Pigeon* to win underlining the genuineness of the National Hunt jockeys. Frank Berry did nothing wrong as JonJo's replacement but the form that has accompanied the latter all year makes me wonder what might have happened had he not fallen on *Grangewood Girl*?

These cases underline the part that falls play in racing — they are completely unpredictable except on the very rare occasions when an animal, bordering on dangerous, appears. Even though every care is taken

A crunching fall

Notification miraculously recovers giving Terry Biddlecombe no chance of 'staying in the plate'. Happily he picks himself up to retrieve his whip from Albert, one of the Sandown Park groundsmen!

Roy Edwards tries to roll clear of the following
Vichyssoise with the eventual winner *Specify* (John
Cook) just last of the leading group at 'The Chair'

Jockey Roy Edwards picks himself up
unhurt after the field has moved on

John Burke and *Royal Frolic* pass the point of no return at the last fence in the 1978 Cheltenham Gold Cup

There are too many steel-shod hooves too close for the fallen jockey's comfort

A bad mistake forces Tim Norman to exit by the 'front door'. Luckily he escapes injury but is none too happy with the outcome

there is only one way to avoid falls, and that is not to ride at all! They are part of the price riders have to pay, though let us not forget that whereas the riders take the risks willingly the horses have no say in the matter.

In fact that is not strictly true, as most jockeys will experience at some stage in their career. Occasionally, despite vigorous encouragement from the rider, a horse's shortening stride together with a rapid deceleration on the approach to an obstacle heralds a refusal. The message is usually quite clear some way before a jump, but in some cases horses have dug their toes in without warning even up to the take-off stride, resulting in the jockey jumping the fence on his own!

Horses' capabilities vary tremendously, and having the honour to have ridden *Pendil* it makes me wonder why all horses do not possess the same magical spring and scope. I suppose if they did, worn out jockeys would still be enjoying the thrill of a steeplechase at fifty years of age instead of opting for easier livings.

Falls occur sometimes because of limited ability, sometimes through bad luck, occasionally from slippery ground conditions but most of all because the pace and lack of room to manoeuvre in a race forces a wrong decision to be made by either or both partners. There are horses which just do not think quickly enough to save themselves, whilst others find a leg when all seems lost. Thankfully the majority of horses try to keep their own backs off the ground, but in doing so often get rid of their jockeys which in the cold light of the next day's results is a slur on the rider's ability. Sadly only those people who witnessed the event realise that no man would have kept the partnership intact. The easiest fall for both parties is when having hit a fence the equine partner fails to put his 'landing gear' down and simply slides along the ground until loss of momentum causes him to gently roll over. Then there is the time when the horse has really put his maximum effort into a leap, the jockey lets the reins slip through his hands allowing his partner to use the full extent of his neck in order to maintain his balance, then should the horse's nose touch the ground (as often happens) his body weight, plus speed forces his head under his front legs. The resultant whiplash sends the rider into orbit. This type of fall surprisingly does little damage to horse or rider, although quite often the followers-on unavoidably finish the job. It never ceases to amaze me, thankfully, how an animal's neck withstands the enormous pressure caused by its half ton weight travelling at speeds of over thirty miles per hour. The real crunch comes when a rider, having a clear view of the jump, mentally counts his last three strides, kicking for take-off at the third stride, only to find for some inexplicable reason the horse has not heeded the aid and has taken a fourth stride which inevitably finishes over the guard rail of the obstacle. The result is a complete upender with the horse at one stage perpendicular to the fence. On these occasions

Chris Read reaches the point of no return as *Daily Mirror* Punters Club horse *Even Up* struggles to keep his feet

Stuart Minsky nose-dives from *Blank Escort*

Walking back with only their pride hurt this time

'Let's get the hell out of here!' Andy Turnell makes the quickest exit possible

Unpleasant wintry conditions cause two horses to fall independently at Lingfield Park

183

Richard Pitman about to fall from *Bee Eater* and Macer Gifford on the floor having fallen from *Charles Dickens* at the Open Ditch in the Mole Handicap Steeplechase at Sandown Park the rider is not thrown far enough away for safety, and it is only luck which decides if the horse engulfs his rider, or falls slightly to one side.

Aintree is a law unto itself with most of the falls resulting from speed and overcrowding early on in the race and tiredness in the later stages. Here, more than anywhere, combinations cannot see what has happened to the horse leading them due to the height of the fences or the drops encountered on many of the landings. It is a weird sensation when a leading horse hits the top of the fence, causing its tail to flick upwards in an effort to regain its balance. Experienced riders know that action indicates a crash, but due to pressure from other runners close by there is often no choice but to launch oneself at the obstacle without really knowing whether the faller has rolled to the left or right, or, as is often the case, is lying directly in the way waiting, albeit unwillingly, to claim a victim.

Any obstacle no matter how small or soft its composition is capable of causing a fall, which nine hundred and ninety nine times out of a thousand means defeat. Riders rarely remount to win though it is by no means impossible. When a young jockey starts out on the stony path to fame, he should not even think of falling when going down to the start. Stan Mellor for

Embarrassing moments for Terry Biddlecombe after fall at Cheltenham

instance remembers riding for at least two years before knowing what a 'Novice Chaser' meant. They were all just rides to him, and he wanted as many of them as he could get. There is, however, a difference between Novice and Handicap Chasers. A fly on the changing room wall before a Novice Chase would relate a definite nervous trend in the pre-race jokes and an excited chatter afterwards — that is from the survivors.

Novices fall more from inexperience, even though they may have schooled well and often at home. It is totally different on the track where the pace is faster, the company not always reliable, and the whole affair creates a new excitement which may cause him to disregard the instructions given by his rider. Nowadays a horse is a Novice Hurdler for the whole of the season in which he wins his first hurdle race, and similarly over fences. So if a horse wins in the early autumn he could still be racing against other novices at the end of that same season, having raced in the meantime against Handicappers.

Hurdle race falls are more dramatic due to the speed with which they happen, plus the likelihood of the field being more closely bunched. Besides the swinging hurdles that act as swiftly and effectively as a trip wire, often horses having smashed through a flight are knocked over by the weight of numbers as they desperately struggle to keep their footing. Riders tend to be thrown much closer to their horses in hurdle races because there is less impact with the obstacle and consequently less difference in the change of speed. Having gone down with his horse, a rider is likely to be rolled on by his partner which looks far worse than it actually is since moving weight bears no relationship to dead weight. Every regular rider must suffer the aggravation of minor setbacks such as broken collar bones, as well as the pain of the important limbs which will be splintered, smashed or simply pulled apart. Jack Dowdeswell who remembers having broken fifty two different bones in his body, had his collar bones removed because in his own words 'It seemed the sensible thing to do, it was a waste of good riding time mending them purely so that I could go out and re-break them.'

Even though every rider knows the crunch is only a question of time, he accepts injury as fair wear and tear, looking forward to the next race as soon as his head hits the hospital pillow! In April 1978, former Champion Jockey Graham Thorner fell at the first hurdle at the Worcester race track, his stumbling mount knocked over by a following horse. As there was little or no height to the fall he ended up under his horse with his feet still in the stirrup irons. Every rider's secret dread is to be hung up by the feet when a horse

Opposite:
First-aid men assist Mr A. MacTaggart at Cheltenham Festival Meeting

Hitting the ground with one boot still in the stirrup iron — the thought of being dragged is every jockey's fear

rises to instinctively gallop after its distant matcs. In Graham's case, as the horse rose the pressure on his leg simply caused it to break. In desperation he snatched at the dangling reins to stop the horse galloping off which actually pulled the animal back on top of him, allowing his twisted leg in the process to fall out of the stirrup. Needless to say he passed out, but when consciousness returned and the sole of his boot was turned up to face him he can remember thinking 'perhaps it was only twisted after all!'

Graham Thorner also sports an attractive dimple on his left cheek which he did not inherit from either parent but it is the result of a particularly horrible fall which smashed his cheek-bones rendering him unrecognisable for many months.

Happily bones mend, given time. However, riders usually insure themselves so that they can afford to have top class private treatment in order to return to the track in the quickest possible time to qualify for the dubious pleasure of being kicked around again once in every ten rides!

I am pleased to say that most times the riders get up,

shake the dust off their breeches and hasten back to relate the happenings to their connections before setting out on another mount. In the 1967 Grand National there was an almighty pile-up at the twenty third fence. Stan Mellor was knocked off his mount *The Fossa* so violently that he himself landed on top of the fence only to see Lord Oaksey (John Lawrence as he was then) sail over the debris without a horse. Both men having been well up with the leaders were only too mindful of the remaining horde behind them, so not wishing to hang around they disentangled themselves and ran like rabbits towards the safety of the far rails. The following day in the *Daily Telegraph* a photograph of both men in full flight appeared, captioned 'S. Mellor and J. Lawrence seen running in search of their mounts.' Both men will vouch that nothing was further from their minds!

Their actions were in the circumstances excusable, but without a doubt the best way to stay in one piece, having fallen, is to roll in a tight ball until you stop and then lie still when every nerve end in your body is screaming at you to 'get the hell out of there', ignore

188

Paul Kelleway falls in the Daily Express Hurdle at Cheltenham 1972

the tumultuous noise and the inescapable knocks, and lastly pray that the big crunch that is accompanied by darkness will not come. Horses in full flight will do everything in their power to miss an object on the floor, even to the extent of stretching again in mid-air. Their chance of missing a fallen rider is less if he is moving.

The amazing thing about falls is that even though the more one has the longer they seem to be, the moment of realisation that another one is actually happening never ceases to come as a surprise. The whole world revolves endlessly, the noise becomes almost unbearable as the field races over the top of a fallen rider with both a shower of kicks and the ground being depressed by steel shod hooves dangerously close to the head. Then when the last runner has gone the beautiful sound of silence is a moment to be cherished. This is usually broken by the welcome words of a member of the St John's Ambulance Brigade saying, 'It's alright now, there is nothing to harm you,' reminding thirty-year-olds of the days when mothers used the same comforting words after a bad nightmare had racked their sleep.

To the laymen, 'fell' and 'fell off' mean the same, but to the jockeys who are a particularly sensitive bunch when it comes to criticism there is a world of difference between them. So when consoling a muddy disappointed jockey please do not say, 'I'm sorry you fell off.' A very pretty girl might get away with it on a fine day when the ground was soft, but from anyone else it is asking for an unprintable reply. Often punters will intimate that a rider who was obviously unseated did so because he did not want to win on that occasion. Let me assure you, if ever those same people had huddled in a ball wondering when a belt from a sledge hammer was going to strike home, they would never glibly use such an accusation again.

For horse and rider the falls are as inevitable as night following day. In the horse's case, the majority suffer little in return for their board and lodging, whilst the riders accept them as part of their job. If you were to ask any medically retired jockey what he would do if he had his time all over again, his answer would most certainly be 'A steeplechase jockey!'

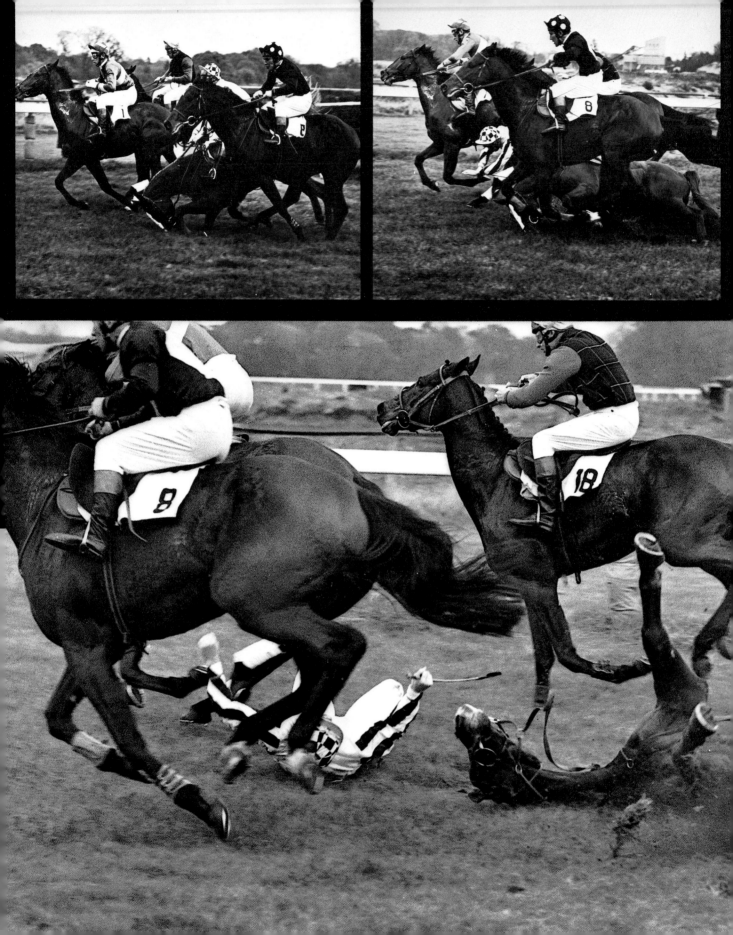

Above:
Even the great Stan Mellor finds the need to correct the last stride of *Log* — but it's all in vain — safe exit 'from the plate'

Top right:
A concussed David Mould

Below right:
Stan Mellor having also fallen, enquires after his fellow jockey's well being

Some of the more unusual and hazardous incidents in steeplechasing

Top left: Landing gear lowered too soon

Above: 'Legs eleven'

Lower left: 'I'm watching you'

Right: 'You won't get rid of me that easily'

Laudon Hall and Richard Pitman completely misjudge Kempton Park's Open Ditch. Amazingly, self-preservation saves the horse whilst his rider records another 'unseated rider' and lives to fight another day.

Trouble starts in the parade ring for Jane Thorne and
Indian Diva and continues in the race. Happily thrown
clear she watches from the safety of the hurdle track as

'Anywhere you go, I'll go!'

10 Reflections on some great horses

Ardent steeplechasing fans often attempt to make comparisons between great horses of different eras — usually the task ends, as it began, with both camps still endeared to their particular hero. The two most outstanding chasers whose merits are stacked one against the other are *Golden Miller* and *Arkle*. Undoubtedly both were great horses and in my mind should remain as the best of their times. It is of little importance which was the better, if indeed that fact could ever be firmly established.

Golden Miller's record time of 9 min 20·4 s when winning the 1934 Grand National with 12 st 2 lb on his back stood for thirty nine years until the legendary Aintree hero *Red Rum* recorded his first victory in the race in 1973 beating the record by 18·5 s. *Red Rum* carried 25 lb less than *Golden Miller* and undoubtedly was forced to beat the record by the fact that the long-time leader and subsequent runner up, *Crisp* (carrying 12 st) maintained such a blistering pace for four of the almost four and a half mile race. This, coupled with Brian Fletcher's persistent driving with hands and heels for the whole of the second circuit, plus the courage that *Red Rum* showed by answering his rider's urging, not only lowered the long-standing record time for the race but also gave the racing world a new hero.

This, it seems, is important for the general health of the sport. People love a winner and the bigger and more frequent the successes the stronger the following. The crowds will flock to see one really good horse in action in preference to supporting a race meeting that has each race filled to the safety limit with nondescript performers. The lesser lights are, however, very necessary to the survival of the sport. The occasional equine that does possess that rare gift 'a fifth gear' has a magical aura surrounding it which binds steeplechasing enthusiasts together in sentiment and conversation.

In recent years *Red Rum* has earned world wide recognition as a result of his three victories and two seconds from his only five attempts at the Grand National. His story has been told many times so there is little point in repeating it now, however, he must figure in these pages because I doubt very much that we will see another horse run five almost identical races over that exacting course. Old stagers will mumble into

their beer mugs about modified fences, agreeing 'fings aint wot they used to be', but let us not forget that neither the height nor the severity of the obstacles has changed. The sole addition is that of a 'belly' on the take-off side which has been added in order to give a horse a ground line, sighted far enough away from the original base to enable a clearance if the animal's stride takes him to the take-off board.

There are many amazing aspects about *Red Rum*'s successes in the Grand National, not least the fact that he was bred to win at distances three and a half miles shorter than the Aintree marathon. The all important 'correct striding' on the approach to a jump comes naturally to him and on the one occasion that his nose did go perilously close to the ground his inbuilt sense of self preservation enabled him to 'find a leg' so quickly that he lost no impetus and precious little ground in the process. Truly a master around Aintree's formidable circuit it is surprising that *Red Rum* has never jumped a proper sized schooling fence off the racecourse, proving once again that he is the exception, not the rule. It was with great interest that watchers saw the tense expression on Beryl McCain's face as *Red Rum* cantered to the post at Haydock Park after racing in February 1978 to school over hurdles with just one stable companion. Secretly the trainer's wife was afraid that *Red Rum* would dig his toes in as he had done at home, but the fact that he was on the racecourse made his adrenalin flow and he played to the gallery, thrilling the large crowd of enthusiasts who had stayed behind to watch him vindicating his trainer's faith and achieving the object of the exercise which was to have a two mile gallop over obstacles as part of Ginger McCain's master plan to obtain peak fitness whilst ensuring the horse's correct state of mind.

Sadly a deep-seated injury to the horse's heel, sustained only ten days before the race, prevented a sixth Aintree attempt despite the best medical attention available. This situation is experienced by trainers throughout the year and curiously enough I think that many of them unknowingly thrive on those

Overleaf:
Arkle with his owner Anne, Duchess of Westminster after winning the Gallagher Gold Cup 1965

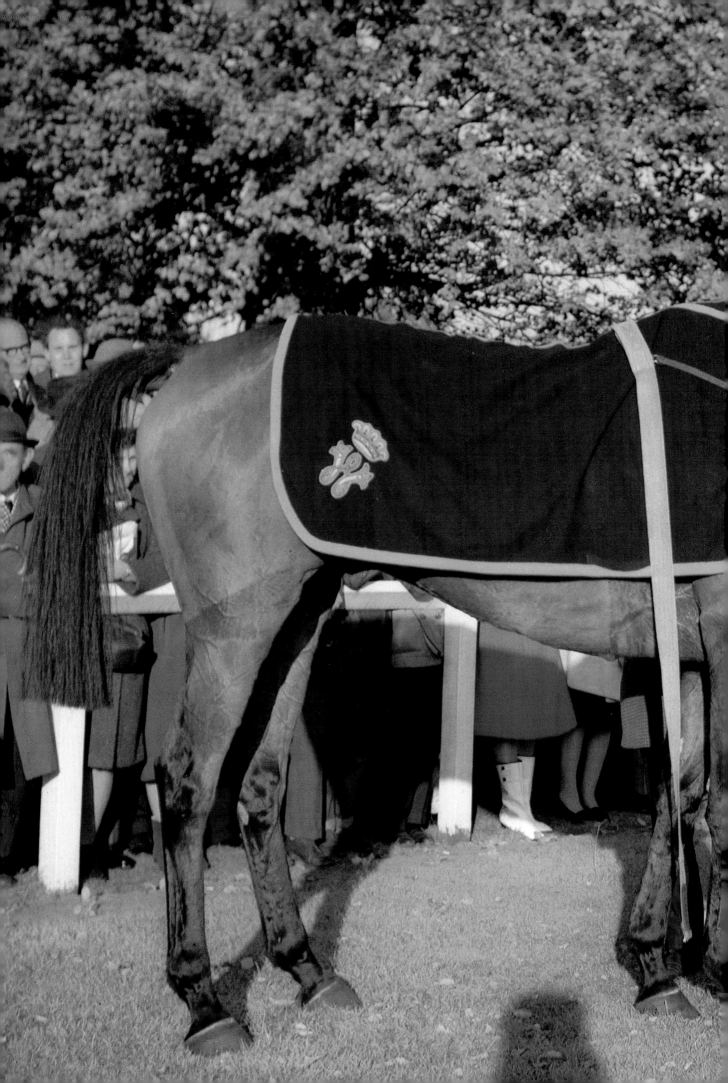

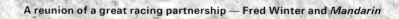
A reunion of a great racing partnership — Fred Winter and *Mandarin*

Arkle after his first victory in the Cheltenham Gold Cup in 1964

'elation to depths of despair' emotions. It is a feat to bring a horse to peak and keep him trouble free let alone to do so for a particular day in the year, and as trainers know only too well 'time waits for no man!'

Always at his best in the Spring, every year *Red Rum* improved in leaps and bounds as each day of March passed until Grand National day when his condition was befitting the parade ring at Royal Ascot. The days of real 'strapping' are long past, but nevertheless horses generally still look a credit to their handlers. A kind, lovable horse, *Red Rum* is extremely ticklish, a condition which transforms him when he is being groomed into a dangerous half ton of horseflesh with snapping teeth at one end and a pair of far reaching hooves at the other. When Billy Beardswood grooms his charge, *Red Rum*'s sole purpose is to rid himself of the cause of his irritation, but within a split second of Billy's body brush breaking contact with *Red Rum*'s skin the handler can stroke his horse's nose or stand immediately behind his hind legs, which only seconds before were intent on sending him into orbit. A great bond is formed between handlers and their horses because of the amount of contact between them, and many of the leading trainers will listen carefully to a stable lad if he detects that something is wrong with his charge, even if he cannot actually pin-point the trouble.

A bronze statue of *Arkle* overlooking the parade ring at Cheltenham erected by the Racegoers Club and unveiled by Anne, Duchess of Westminster accompanied by Tom Dreaper

Red Rum, now doing the rounds as a personality has many years in this capacity to play to the crowds, and like all great stars, both human and animal, he visibly takes pleasure in their applause. Many people think that racehorses deserve a quiet paddock to live in when their competitive days are over, but *Red Rum* has been used to the best food money can buy, regular exercise, warm clothing and accommodation, plus the daily attention of a loving groom, and I am sure he would opt for his present job if only he could talk.

In terms of actual racing ability to find the best racehorse that has graced the tracks since the Second World War we must go back to the mid sixties when the Duchess of Westminster's *Arkle* held the stage. It was not just his three consecutive Cheltenham Gold Cups, two Hennessy Gold Cups, and victories in the King George VI, Irish Grand National and the Whitbread Gold Cup, or his other eighteen victories that made him great, it was his style in accomplishing it. So popular a hero was he that wherever he went any Irishman worth his salt would refer to the equine athlete by saying 'T'is himself' — surely there can be no greater compliment. So good was he that it was only on the occasions when the handicapper set him impossible weight differences against horses that were themselves

The good honest head of the Australian chaser *Crisp* in his Lambourn stable

in Gold Cup class, that he was defeated, and then always with honour.

Handled by that genius the late Tom Dreaper, *Arkle* was not purely potential, he was the ultimate. To race against him was soul destroying for other jockeys and heart breaking for their equine partners. His jumping was fast, clean, deadly accurate and probably most important he was extremely swift away from obstacles. In his 'pilot', Pat Taaffe, he had a man that was the very definition of a horseman. His eye for a stride was uncanny as was his judge of pace, and on the one occasion that *Arkle* did hit a solid Cheltenham fence half-way up, Pat Taaffe remained unmoved even though everyone in the packed grandstand instinctively gasped for breath and found their hearts pounding at twice the normal rate.

At first it was with total disbelief that Englishmen accepted *Arkle*'s possible superiority over *Mill House*, but time proved him to be so and because racing people appreciate the best they soon identified themselves with him as a British horse. Throughout steeplechasing history there have been many horses which would have been great but for continually clashing with one superior rival. This was the case with *Mill House* who took a Gold Cup at Cheltenham as well as the Whitbread, Hennessy and King George VI Chase. *Arkle* put so much into his races that it would not have been a surprise to learn that his engine had burned out, but fate decided instead that a cracked pedal bone in his hoof was to be his undoing. The pedal bone is the central bone of the foot taking incalculable pressure each time a horse lands over a jump at the speeds *Arkle* was capable of. Although attended constantly by Irish veterinary surgeon, Maxi Cosgrove, *Arkle* never appeared on the race track afterwards, though he was trained for some time in the hopes of a comeback. If you have never witnessed any of his races it is hard to realise his brilliance, but a comparison can be drawn with Bjorn Borg's third Wimbledon single's title over Jimmy Connors in 1978. A champion beating another convincingly!

So it is that every top class chaser since *Arkle* has invariably been measured by his standards, and try as we may, we eventually have to accept for one reason or another that as yet we have not found his equal.

Golden Miller was an incredible horse, winning twenty nine races in all. He was bred from an ex-hunting mare by a five guinea Irish stallion and he dominated the Cheltenham Gold Cup in the 1930s —

Top right:
Arkle leads *Mill House* at the open ditch in Sandown Park's Gallagher Gold Cup 1965

Lower right:
Comedy of Errors the highest prize money winner over hurdles

Dual Cheltenham Gold Cup and Grand National winner, *L'Escargot*, with his regular partner Tommy Carberry

The head of a legend — *Red Rum*

Prolific winner *Captain Christy* with his trainer, Pat Taaffe

winning in five successive years from 1932 to 1936. *Golden Miller* was owned by the eccentric Hon. Dorothy Paget and ridden mainly by Gerry Wilson who was Fred Rimell's brother-in-law.

Two modern-day chasers who have come close to matching *Arkle*'s achievements are *Captain Christy* who was trained by *Arkle*'s jockey Pat Taaffe, and *Pendil* trained by Fred Winter.

About 10 lb below the crack hurdlers, *Pendil*'s style of jumping fences from the very first schooling session sent a wave of excitement through the stable. He was experienced as far as jumping was concerned before the end of that first morning — he was a 'natural'. In fact *Pendil* was so brilliant that it was frightening to even think about his prospects. In the end it was his vast superiority that cost him his short head defeat in the 1973 Gold Cup and a combination of events that cut him down a year later. His one quirk was a complete disinterest in a race after he had hit the front, but usually the opposition had fired all their guns by the time *Pendil* started to idle so he won comfortably enough without racing over the final few furlongs.

This same thing happened at Cheltenham, incredibly still pulling for his head as the field swept around the final bend with just two fences to jump, *Pendil* settled the issue in two ground-devouring strides, urged to do so by his competitive instincts instead of his jockey's decision. The way he did accelerate in a race of such importance was indicative of a truly great horse, endorsing his earlier shows of brilliance when winning over distances from two to three miles. Although thought by many racing scribes to be at his best around Kempton Park's sharp circuit, the 'feel' that *Pendil* gave me at Newbury and Cheltenham on numerous occasions convinced me that he was extraordinary. It was also a popular theory that *Pendil* did not quite stay the three and a quarter miles of the 1973 Gold Cup, but I shall go to my grave knowing that he did stay every inch of the trip.

Having arrived at the second last fence in the 1973 Gold Cup in front I decided to let *Pendil* run, knowing full well that it was too soon but hoping that his superiority would bring him the Gold Cup despite his usual switching off habit. On reflection I should have asked for a 'long one' at the last fence instead of letting *Pendil* jump it in his normal stride, since two hundred yards later I needed only six inches to win Fred Winter his first Cheltenham Gold Cup, and had I chosen to ask for the 'long one' at the last fence I could have gained ten feet in the air.

Had he not possessed so much speed he would not have hit the front rounding the final bend, delivering his challenge hopefully after the last fence and struggling to take the spoils rather than going away from the final fence with the race sewn up with the result that he froze at the sight and sound of his own supporters.

The simple answer to *Pendil*'s defeat lay with his jockey for allowing his mount to arrive on the scene too soon. Had he waited to use his speed until after the last fence then *Pendil*'s fans would undoubtedly have witnessed the most impressive winner of the race since *Arkle*. The short head winner, *The Dikler*, was a graduate from the point-to-point field, sired by that prolific winner *Vulgan*, who without fail passed on jumping ability to all his progeny. It was a sweet victory for *The Dikler* fans who had suffered severe blows to their arguments on previous meetings, and sweeter still for his handler Darkie Deacon and trainer Fulke Walwyn who operates his business next to Fred Winter's stableyard in Lambourn. Walwyn is of course no stranger to the winners' enclosure, and has consistently turned out major race winners throughout his long and honourable career, proving in the process that good horses come in all shapes and sizes.

The Dikler and *Mill House* were big individuals whereas his 1964 Grand National winner *Team Spirit* was quite small as was *Mandarin* who won a King George VI Chase, two Hennessy Gold Cups and the 1962 Cheltenham Gold Cup. However the race which will stick in every Frenchman's mind and those of the British enthusiasts who were fortunate enough to witness first hand the bond between man and his horse, was the 1962 French Grand National. Ridden by Fred Winter, *Mandarin* obeyed each instruction that his rider gave him, and in this case more than any other recorded horse race, every decision had to be the right one. Run at Auteill, the race criss-crosses and even returns on the part of the course where it started but in the opposite direction. Imagine Fred Winter's reactions when after only a third of the race had progressed he felt and then saw that *Mandarin*'s bridle had broken. The bit dangled uselessly from his mount's mouth leaving him without a means of either stopping or steering. It is amazing, but often the case, that when a horse's bluff is called it is lost for action. *Mandarin* was a hard pulling horse usually and with no bit in his mouth you would assume that he would take charge, careering off in front of the field. In fact the opposite happened, he seemed content to stay with the leaders in a far more relaxed state than was normal. About five fences from home this complex course split into three with small privet hedges lining each course. At this point the partnership were in third place just off the leading two horses who bore left-handed on the correct track. *Mandarin* seeing them turn followed suit, but at that time he had not cleared the entrance to one of the other two tracks and so was destined to take the wrong course. The little bay had actually started his turn when Fred Winter changed his direction purely by throwing his own bodyweight in the opposite direction without, I may add, falling off from his own momentum. It was a most fantastic riding feat, and he then proceeded to urge his gallant mount past the

Night Nurse — the great front running hurdler

winning post to hold on by a neck to record a fairy-tale victory.

Unfortunately leg trouble has put paid to many good horses, *Captain Christy* being no exception. He was first noticed at Cheltenham's festival meeting ridden by his owner Major Joe Pidcock who had attained the age of reason some fifty years previously but like so many cavaliers put the joy of riding at speed over obstacles before his personal safety. The Major often steered an erratic course through a race which was mainly due to his liking for hard pulling horses combined with a determination to hold them in the pack. Comments from jockeys in the races were showered upon the Major who appeared either unperturbed or hard of hearing. During his first race at Cheltenham *Captain Christy*'s race pattern was far from regular as his intrepid rider tried to hold him back with varying degrees of success. Having seen the front on the wide outside several times and still in contention when the runners swept for home, several reliable race readers noted him for the future. They were correct in their assessment, the Major sold him to Mrs Pat Samuel who watched him win the Irish Sweeps Hurdle in 1972 before going on to take two consecutive wins in the King George VI Chase in 1974 and 1975 and the Cheltenham Gold Cup in 1974.

His steeplechase victories were show-stoppers for different reasons. When he won the Gold Cup he beat the previous year's winner *The Dikler* despite a bad mistake at the last fence which showed the racing world that the brilliant jockey and stylist Bobby Beasley had made a successful comeback. The cheers that surrounded the unsaddling enclosure were louder than usual as even those punters who had lost their money felt a joy in being a part of this success. *Pendil* had been brought down three fences from home when going tremendously well and as disappointed as I was, those cheers for Bobby and *Captain Christy* sounded good.

Ten weeks earlier *Captain Christy* partnered by Bobby Coonan had left the Kempton Park crowd gasping and myself with a very red face, when he set off in the King George VI Chase as if the devil was after him. In fact no one was after him, because I was convinced that *Captain Christy* was a bad jumper and would certainly not get round at worst or at best he would make a hash of things which would inevitably force me to be in front on *Pendil* long before I wanted to be there. Neither happened, and image the panic that swept through me when I pressed the button to go and found that I had used *Pendil*'s reserves purely to get into the race. *Captain Christy* strode away to record

209

a flying, foot perfect victory hammering home a lesson that Fred Winter had long advocated, 'You cannot afford to give a good horse a start; if you wish to hold your mount up for a late run, jump out of the gate smartly and then settle back to a comfortable position with the opposition always in the sights.' Those words of wisdom have echoed through my head many times since then. The following year although aware of his front running intention the runners headed by dual Champion Hurdler *Bula* could never get a blow in once the first fence had been jumped and *Captain Christy* stormed home again in truly great style. His legs let him down before the Gold Cup which was racing's loss as well as his connections'. However, one man's meat is another man's poison, and *Captain Christy*'s non-participation left the way clear for *Arkle*'s owner to take the race with *Ten Up* in conditions which Irishmen would call good jumping ground but which the stewards of the meeting called unraceable and accordingly abandoned the remainder of the card.

In 1978 Fred Winter won his first Gold Cup with Mrs Olive Jackson's *Midnight Court* whose main opposition was his neighbour's candidate *Fort Devon*.

The star hurdler *Night Nurse* with Paddy Broderick up gives an exhibition of fast clean jumping

As *Midnight Court* was only seven years old then, he has time to make his mark amongst the truly great steeplechasers. He improved throughout the season maintaining his peak despite the fact that his real goal was delayed by a month. This was because after the first two days of the Gold Cup meeting, amazed participants awoke on the third day to find six inches of snow covering the course. True, the month's delay before the race could be run was the same for all the horses, although some would obviously take it better than others. *Fort Devon* at the age of twelve had run some really good trials, not least his neck defeat in the Hennessy Gold Cup by Peter Cundell's *Bachelor's Hall* to whom he was giving a stone in weight. As the Gold Cup progressed watchers could see John Francome poised behind the leaders riding his usual waiting race, ready to pounce when he thought fit. John, however, was far from happy as the field breasted the hill, but sharp slaps down his mount's shoulder changed the situation dramatically as he slipped into overdrive. *Fort Devon* led into the last bend with the 1976 winner *Royal Frolic* on his outside, the pair racing some two yards off the running rail. This temptation was the signal for Francome to make his challenge and so fast did he slip through the gap that Bill Smith had no time

Two great rival hurdling partnerships of the early 1970s
— Fred Winter and *Lanzarote* (*left*), *Comedy of Errors*
and Fred Rimell (*right*)

to close it, and within the space of two strides the Gold
Cup was safe in Fred Winter's hands. The last fence
proved no problem to *Midnight Court* whereas ten
lengths behind him *Royal Frolic* completely misjudged
his take-off, suffering a really nasty fall as a result,
whilst *Fort Devon* suffered a broken blood-vessel which
accounted for his somewhat quiet finish. But as
Midnight Court passed the very spot where *Pendil*
faltered on the run-in five years previously, he did a
similar thing, freezing at the sight of the crowds and
supporters, although happily his lead was sufficient to
make little difference to the result.

The month's delay meant that *Fort Devon* missed his
intended run in the Grand National although in the
light of his blood-vessel trouble that may have been a
blessing in disguise. Hopefully we will see this
American owned, Irish bred and English trained
chestnut participate in the Aintree marathon in 1979.
He has class enough to carry what is sure to be a
formidable weight and the nearest style of jumping to
Red Rum's that I have seen. Some way before an
obstacle *Fort Devon* pricks his ears as he weighs the
situation up, and then proceeds to adjust his footwork
in order to meet the jump on a good stride. This style of
jumping lends itself to a safe passage around Aintree
and as *Fort Devon* was a late developing animal his age
of thirteen years should not be against him.

If chasing is the ideal that we aim for, the
kindergarten — hurdling, — certainly provides as
many heroes and interesting duels between them. The
bulk of the timber toppers start their career at three
or four years of age, with obvious chasing types
graduating to the larger obstacles at the ideal age of six.
The hurdlers that show above average form delay their
chasing débuts in favour of a chance at either the
Champion Hurdle or one of the many valuable
handicaps that now span the season. However, it is the
popular belief that the good horses which stay hurdling
longer than the initial education stage are not able to
adapt to jumping the larger obstacles when their
superiority over timber ends. Certainly up to now that
is true as there has been no Champion Hurdler which
has gone on to win a Gold Cup, although I am sure the
time will come before very long.

So far three horses have won the title of Champion
Hurdler on three occasions and each of those did it in
consecutive years. From 1949 to 1951 inclusive, the
crown was the property of *Hatton's Grace* trained by
the now all-conquering flat trainer Vincent O'Brien
and from 1952 to 1954, *Sir Ken* trained at Royston by
Willie Stephenson. After that, the title went to thirteen
individual horses until the Colin Davies trained
Persian War took it on three consecutive occasions
(1968 to 1970) following his victory in the juvenile
crown the previous year. In fact he is the only Triumph
Hurdle winner to have gone on to take the adult title,
though *Monksfield* almost did the double, being foiled
by *Peterhof* in the Triumph Hurdle. These top hurdlers

seem to maintain their peak for three years but it always comes as a surprise when the time comes for them to be deposed.

Persian War's victories were thrilling to watch and in his rider he had one of our most stylish jockeys, Jimmy Uttley. The winner of a couple of minor flat races *Persian War* was then physically not mature enough to be the good horse he was bred to be. His powerful frame spurred on by a brave heart were the attributes that endeared him to the vast crowds who watched him forge up the Cheltenham hill, although it did take him some time to learn to pick his feet up when he came to a hurdle. As a juvenile he flattened many an obstacle without losing any momentum or giving away any ground, but by the time he was in his second season he had well and truly got the message.

Although he was at one time considered chasing material, *Persian War* did not actually grace the chase course with his presence. His reign was ended by a gelding, bred for the jumping game who was considered slow in home gallops, but whose late finishes accompanied by a continual tail swishing action commanded a large following — his name was *Bula*. Bought by Martin Malony for Fred Winter, *Bula* did not even impress Brian Delaney, Winter's head lad, on his arrival at Uplands. His daily record still bears the proof it read: 'Common looking gelding arrived, top heavy and don't like its front legs!' The lads were also not impressed and no one particularly wanted to take him under their wing, although in the end Vince Brookes accepted him along with *Pendil* as his two to look after. I think that good lads are a considerable contributory factor relating to the success of a racehorse especially when they ride their charges at daily exercise as well as tending to their stable needs.

Bula never did his best at home having fathomed out each different gallop soon after his arrival, but the schooling sessions had the reverse effect turning him into a little fireball which at least gave all concerned a glimmer of hope. He was ridden to most of his hurdle victories by Paul Kelleway who was indeed a cool customer. Paul liked to switch *Bula* off completely, in a race, by settling the son of *Raincheck* behind the whole field, allowing him to idle along until the last half mile of the race when he would ask *Bula* to show his paces, which he did by winning twenty one of his twenty six hurdle races including the 1971 Champion Hurdle, when he ended *Persian War*'s supremacy by four well earned lengths. Paul maintained that *Bula* had only two gears — idle and full power — and if asked to lay up with the leaders in a race would burn himself out. On many occasions Paul would give Fred Winter and Captain Edwards-Heathcote cause for alarm as he waited at the back of the field long after the connections in the grandstand had mentally urged him to make a forward move. However, he knew his mount inside out and would return triumphantly to the

unsaddling enclosure exhibiting his famous lop sided grin, saying, 'Never in danger of defeat!' This horse was a prime example of employing the correct tactics to obtain the best results and in this sphere the top trainers excell. *Bula* retained his title in 1972 in breathtaking style, but was knocked off his perch the following year by *Comedy of Errors*. Two years later in 1975 he went to Cheltenham as the winner of eight of his ten steeplechases and a warm favourite to become the first Champion Hurdler to win the Gold Cup. In hock-deep ground he finished third to *Ten Up*, after making a bone-shuddering mistake at the last fence, as did his stable companion the American bred and owned *Soothsayer*. Both horses were nearly stationary on landing but with the subconscious inbuilt drive that true chasers possess they both gave more than their all and struggled to the line. I must admit to the fact that John Francome's presence beside me in the race gave me that extra inspiration that forced *Soothsayer*, my mount, up on the line to take second place. It was the age old fact of the teacher finding his pupil in charge since for the first time I had recorded less winners than the previous season and John, my understudy, had recorded more. He was at that time a better jockey than I had ever been and in the last three years has improved to his present high standard.

Sadly *Bula* suffered a shoulder injury in the 1977 National Hunt Two Mile Champion Chase which led to the need to destroy him. On reflection this great horse did not quite have the stamina to get the three and a quarter miles of the Gold Cup against Gold Cup opposition, although he could do so easily against lesser lights. His conqueror in the 1973 Champion Hurdle, *Comedy of Errors* was sired by the sprinter *Goldhill* and although he went on to stay two and three quarter miles he still retained the speed his father had passed on to him and was able to win a Champion Hurdle at two miles. As mentioned earlier, because of the length of a jumper's career, great protracted duels develop and during the time of *Comedy of Errors* his constant thorn was Lord Howard de Walden's *Lanzarote*. There was precious little between them though *Comedy of Errors* did manage to come out on top in all but the 1974 Champion Hurdle when he had to settle for second place. Initially the two trainers, Fred Rimell and Fred Winter kept their charges apart leaving the decider to the Champion Hurdle itself, and again the racing world was split in two but at least 50 per cent of the fans must have gone home satisfied. One happy aspect of their rivalry was the goodwill between the trainers who agreed the victor would buy the vanquished a bottle of champagne whenever their horses clashed. Fred Winter was the recipient more times than Fred Rimell, but would have gladly reversed the roles.

Comedy of Errors is a huge horse and was best when held up for late challenge with a tendency to hang right-handed when under pressure which makes his two Champion Hurdles even greater considering the Cheltenham course runs left-handed. He was owned by Ted Wheatley and his business partner Harold Plotnek. Originally bought by Fred Rimell on Ted's instructions as a present of gratitude for his partner, but so highly did the trainer regard his purchase that he persuaded Ted to give Harold a half share and as the saying goes 'half a loaf is better than none!' This loaf turned out to be the winner of approximately £96 000 in first prize money and had his connections decided to persevere over fences they would surely have topped the £100 000 mark. Happily they decided to retire him having read the warning signs of impending leg trouble and are to be congratulated for doing so. He now teams up with Mercy Rimell at daily exercise and a handsome pair they are!

Unfortunately *Lanzarote* had to be destroyed after falling in his attempt to win the Gold Cup, having been the Champion Hurdler in 1974, and so the stage is set for *Night Nurse* to attempt the feat. *Lanzarote* excelled around Kempton's right-handed track, being undefeated on the only eight occasions he started there. His inbuilt racing instinct made him accelerate the moment he met the running rail that guides the runners around the long final bend. It was as if he were actually racing the rails themselves, a feeling of power to the rider that is seldom felt and once experienced, never forgotten. Having won the Champion Hurdle by forcing tactics it was thought that it was the correct way to ride him, but we found out differently and reversed the orders again. This as previously stated is where a jockey/trainer relationship is important, they must be able to converse, knowing what is needed and have the guts to change an accepted pattern. A 'yes man' will never last long in steeplechasing, likewise someone who is too dogmatic to change even if they think it would be for the best.

So the cycle goes on and the last two champions *Night Nurse* and the entire, *Monksfield* have both demonstrated courage to the 'Nth' degree. For two years *Night Nurse* held court and even defied adverse ground conditions to record his second triumph in the Champion Hurdle, but in 1978 the previous year's runner up *Monksfield* asserted his authority at Cheltenham before hammering home the truth at Aintree in the Templegate Hurdle, a race which they had dead-heated for twelve months earlier. The respective horses are destined for totally different careers, *Night Nurse* takes on the bigger obstacles whilst *Monksfield* is prepared for another campaign over hurdles with a stud career as his eventual reward for services rendered to hurdling.

The two-mile chasers are exciting but they do not attract the same following as the Gold Cup heroes. Home bred *Royal Relief* won the championship twice and was placed every other year he contested it, and the Irish have taken the prize home on twelve occasions in the last twenty years, but by far the most exciting two-mile star was Colonel Bill Whitbread's *Dunkirk* who was tried at three miles only to give his all against the mighty *Arkle* at Kempton Park, and in his case his all literally was his life.

I close this protracted interpretation of our sport with an excerpt from Timeform's *Chasers and Hurdlers of 1976/77.*

'The price paid for the almost unrivalled spectacle of steeplechasing and hurdling is exceptionally high. Some riders and very many horses have died as a result of accidents on the course over the years; serious injury to both rider and horse is sadly, but unavoidably, virtually an everyday occurrence during a season. In the 1976/77 season more than one hundred and fifty horses were killed in action mostly as a result of a fall. The majority were not leading lights, but some did possess ability considerably above average and like *Lanzarote*, were types racing could ill afford to lose. Accepting and adjusting to the sudden loss of a prominent jumper year after year is a distressing part of being a follower of the sport, but to accept and adjust does not necessarily mean to erase from the memory.'

11 Statistics

Red Rum with Brian Fletcher up, matches strides with *L'Escargot* and Tommy Carberry at the last fence in the 1975 Grand National

GRAND NATIONAL

Held at Aintree, Liverpool — a steeplechase over 4 miles 856 yards (In 1916, 1917 and 1918 the race was held at Gatwick in Surrey)

WINNERS

Year	Winner	Age	Weight (st-lb)	Jockey	Starting Price	Runners
1837*	The Duke	a		Mr Potts		4
1838*	Sir Henry	a		T. Oliver		10
1839	Lottery	a	12-0	J. Mason	5-1	17
1840	Jerry	a	12-0	B. Bretherton	12-1	13
1841	Charity	a	12-0	Powell	14-1	10
1842	Gay Lad	a	12-0	T. Oliver	7-1	15
1843	Vanguard	a	11-10	T. Oliver	12-1	16
1844	Discount	a	10-12	Crickmere	5-1	16
1845	Cureall	a	11-5	W. Loft		15
1846	Pioneer	6	11-12	Taylor		22
1847	Matthew	a	10-6	D. Wynne	10-11	28
1848	Chandler	a	11-12	Capt Little	12-1	29
1849	Peter Simple	a	11-0	T. Cunningham	20-1	23
1850	Abd-el-Kader	a	9-12	C. Green		32
1851	Abd-el-Kader	a	10-4	T. Abbott	7-1	21
1852	Miss Mowbray	a	10-4	Mr A. Goodman		24
1853	Peter Simple	a	10-10	T. Oliver	9-1	21
1854	Bourton	a	11-12	Tasker	4-1	20
1855	Wanderer	a	9-8	J. Hanlon	25-1	20
1856	Free Trader	a	9-6	G. Stevens	25-1	21
1857	Emigrant	a	9-10	C. Boyce	10-1	28
1858	Little Charlie	a	10-7	W. Archer	100-6	16
1859	Half Caste	6	9-7	C. Green	7-1	16
1860	Anatis	a	9-10	Mr Thomas	7-2	19
1861	Jealousy	a	9-12	J. Kendall	5-1	24
1862	Huntsman	a	11-0	H. Lamplugh	3-1	13
1863	Emblem	a	10-10	G. Stevens	4-1	16
1864	Emblematic	6	10-6	G. Stevens	10-1	25
1865	Alcibiade	5	11-4	Capt Coventry	100-7	23
1866	Salamander	a	10-7	Mr A. Goodman	40-1	30
1867	Cortolvin	a	11-13	J. Page	10-6	23
1868	The Lamb	6	10-7	Mr Edwards	10-1	21
1869	The Colonel	6	10-7	G. Stevens	13-1	22
1870	The Colonel	7	11-12	G. Stevens	4-1	23
1871	The Lamb	a	11-4	Mr Thomas	5-1	25
1872	Casse Tete	a	10-0	J. Page	20-1	25
1873	Disturbance	6	11-11	Mr J. Richardson	20-1	28
1874	Reugny	6	10-12	Mr J. Richardson	5-1	22
1875	Pathfinder	a	10-11	Mr Thomas	100-6	19
1876	Regal	5	11-3	J. Cannon	25-1	19
1877	Austerlitz	5	10-8	Mr E. Hobson	15-1	16
1878	Shifnal	a	10-12	J. Jones	7-1	12
1879	Liberator	a	11-4	Mr G. Moore	5-1	18

Year	Winner	Age	Weight (st-lb)	Jockey	Starting Price	Runners
1880	Empress	5	10-7	Mr T. Beasley	8-1	14
1881	Woodbrook	7	11-3	Mr T. Beasley	6-1	13
1882	Seaman	6	11-6	Lord Manners	10-1	12
1883	Zoedone	6	11-0	Count C. Kinsky	100-8	10
1884	Voluptuary	6	10-5	Mr E. Wilson	10-1	15
1885	Roquefort	6	11-0	Mr E. Wilson	100-30	19
1886	Old Joe	7	10-9	T. Skelton	25-1	23
1887	Gamecock	8	11-0	W. Daniells	20-1	16
1888	Playfair	7	10-7	Mawson	40-1	20
1889	Frigate	11	11-5	Mr T. Beasley	8-1	20
1890	Ilex	6	10-5	A. Nightingall	4-1	16
1891	Come Away	7	11-12	Mr H. Beasley	4-1	21
1892	Father O'Flynn	7	10-5	Capt R. Owen	20-1	25
1893	Cloister	9	12-7	Dollery	9-2	15
1894	Why Not	13	11-3	A. Nightingall	5-1	16
1895	Wild Man From Borneo	7	10-1	Mr J. Widger	10-1	19
1896	The Soarer	a	9-13	Mr D. Campbell	40-1	28
1897	Manifesto	9	11-3	T. Kavanagh	6-1	28
1898	Drogheda	6	10-12	J. Gourley	25-1	25
1899	Manifesto	11	12-7	G. Williamson	5-1	19
1900	Ambush II	6	11-3	A. Anthony	4-1	16
1901	Grudon	11	10-0	A. Nightingall	9-1	24
1902	Shannon Lass	7	10-1	D. Read	20-1	21
1903	Drumcree	9	11-3	P. Woodland	13-2	23
1904	Moifaa	8	10-7	A. Birch	25-1	26
1905	Kirkland	9	11-5	F. Mason	6-1	25
1906	Ascetic's Silver	9	10-9	Hon. A. Hastings	20-1	23
1907	Eremon	7	10-1	A. Newey	8-1	23
1908	Rubio	10	10-5	H. Bletsoe	66-1	24
1909	Lutteur III	5	10-11	G. Parfremont	100-9	32
1910	Jenkinstown	9	10-5	R. Chadwick	100-8	25
1911	Glenside	9	10-3	Mr J. Anthony	20-1	20
1912	Jerry M	9	12-7	E. Piggott	4-1	22
1913	Covercoat	7	11-6	P. Woodland	100-9	22
1914	Sunloch	8	9-7	W. Smith	100-6	20
1915	Ally Sloper	6	10-6	Mr J. Anthony	100-8	20
1916	Vermouth	6	11-10	J. Reardon	100-8	21
1917	Ballymacad	10	9-12	E. Driscoll	100-9	19
1918	Poethlyn	8	11-6	E. Piggott	5-1	17
1919	Poethlyn	9	12-7	E. Piggott	11-4	22
1920	Troytown	7	11-9	Mr J. Anthony	6-1	24
1921	Shaun Spadah	10	11-7	F. Rees	100-9	35
1922	Music Hall	9	11-8	L. Rees	100-9	32

Year	Winner	Age	Weight (st-lb)	Jockey	Starting Price	Runners
1923	Sergeant Murphy	13	11-3	Capt G. Bennett	100-6	27
1924	Master Robert	11	10-5	R. Trudgill	25-1	31
1925	Double Chance	9	10-9	Maj J. Wilson	100-9	33
1926	Jack Horner	9	10-5	W. Watkinson	25-1	30
1927	Sprig	10	12-4	T. E. Leader	8-1	37
1928	Tipperary Tim	10	10-0	Mr W. P. Dutton	100-1	42
1929	Gregalach	7	11-4	R. Everett	100-1	66
1930	Shaun Goilin	10	11-0	T. Cullinan	100-8	41
1931	Grakle	9	11-7	R. Lyall	100-6	43
1932	Forbra	7	10-7	J. Hamey	50-1	36
1933	Kellsboro' Jack	7	11-9	D. Williams	25-1	34
1934	Golden Miller	7	12-2	G. Wilson	8-1	30
1935	Reynoldstown	8	11-4	Mr F. Furlong	22-1	27
1936	Reynoldstown	9	12-2	Mr F. Walwyn	10-1	35
1937	Royal Mail	8	11-13	E. Williams	100-6	33
1938	Battleship	11	11-6	B. Hobbs	40-1	36
1939	Workman	9	10-6	T. Hyde	100-8	37
1940	Bogskar	7	10-4	M. Jones	25-1	30
1941-45	No race					
1946	Lovely Cottage	9	10-8	Capt R. Petre	25-1	34
1947	Caughoo	8	10-0	E. Dempsey	100-1	57
1948	Sheila's Cottage	9	10-7	A. Thompson	50-1	43
1949	Russian Hero	9	10-8	L. McMorrow	66-1	43
1950	Freebooter	9	11-11	J. Power	10-1	49
1951	Nickel Coin	9	10-1	J. Bullock	40-1	36
1952	Teal	10	10-12	A. Thompson	100-7	47

Year	Winner	Age	Weight (st-lb)	Jockey	Starting Price	Runners
1953	Early Mist	8	11-2	B. Marshall	20-1	32
1954	Royal Tan	10	11-7	B. Marshall	8-1	29
1955	Quare Times	9	11-0	P. Taaffe	100-9	30
1956	E.S.B.	10	11-3	D. Dick	100-7	29
1957	Sundew	11	11-7	F. Winter	20-1	35
1958	Mr. What	8	10-6	A. Freeman	18-1	31
1959	Oxo	8	10-13	M. Scudamore	8-1	34
1960	Merryman II	9	10-12	G. Scott	13-2	26
1961	Nicolaus Silver	9	10-1	H. Beasley	28-1	35
1962	Kilmore	12	10-4	F. Winter	28-1	32
1963	Ayala	9	10-0	P. Buckley	66-1	47
1964	Team Spirit	12	10-3	W. Robinson	18-1	33
1965	Jay Trump	8	11-5	Mr C. Smith	100-6	47
1966	Anglo	8	10-0	T. Norman	50-1	47
1967	Foinavon	9	10-0	J. Buckingham	100-1	47
1968	Red Alligator	9	10-0	B. Fletcher	100-7	45
1969	Highland Wedding	12	10-4	E. Harty	100-9	30
1970	Gay Trip	8	11-5	P. Taaffe	15-1	28
1971	Specify	9	10-13	J. Cook	28-1	38
1972	Well To Do	9	10-1	G. Thorner	14-1	42
1973	Red Rum	8	10-5	B. Fletcher	9-1	38
1974	Red Rum	9	12-0	B. Fletcher	11-1	42
1975	L'Escargot	12	11-3	T. Carberry	13-2	31
1976	Rag Trade	10	10-12	J. Burke	14-1	32
1977	Red Rum	12	11-8	T. Stack	9-1	42
1978	Lucius	9	10-9	R. Davies	14-1	37

*Considered by some authorities to have been the original 'Grand Nationals', but by others to have been held at Maghull   a = aged   — often used at one time for horses 7 years old or over

MOST WINS

Horses

Red Rum 1973, 1974, 1977 (also 2nd in 1975, 1971)
Peter Simple 1849, 1853
Abd-el-Kader 1850, 1851
The Lamb 1868, 1871
The Colonel 1869, 1870
Manifesto 1897, 1899 (also 3rd in 1900, 1902, 1903)
Poethlyn 1918, 1919 (1918 at Gatwick)
Reynoldstown 1935, 1936

Owners

Captain Henry Machell — Disturbance 1873, Reugny 1874, Regal 1876
Sir Charles Assheton-Smith (formerly Charles Duff) — Cloister 1893, Jerry M 1912, Covercoat 1913

Trainers

Fred Rimell — E.S.B. 1956, Nicolaus Silver 1961, Gay Trip 1970, Rag Trade 1976
Hon. Aubrey Hastings — Ascetic's Silver 1906, Ally Sloper 1915, Master Robert 1924, Ballymacad 1917 (at Gatwick)

FASTEST TIME

9 min. 01·9 sec Red Rum 1973

SMALLEST FIELD

10 in 1841 and 1883 (apart from the Maghull races in 1837 and 1838)

LARGEST FIELD

66 in 1929

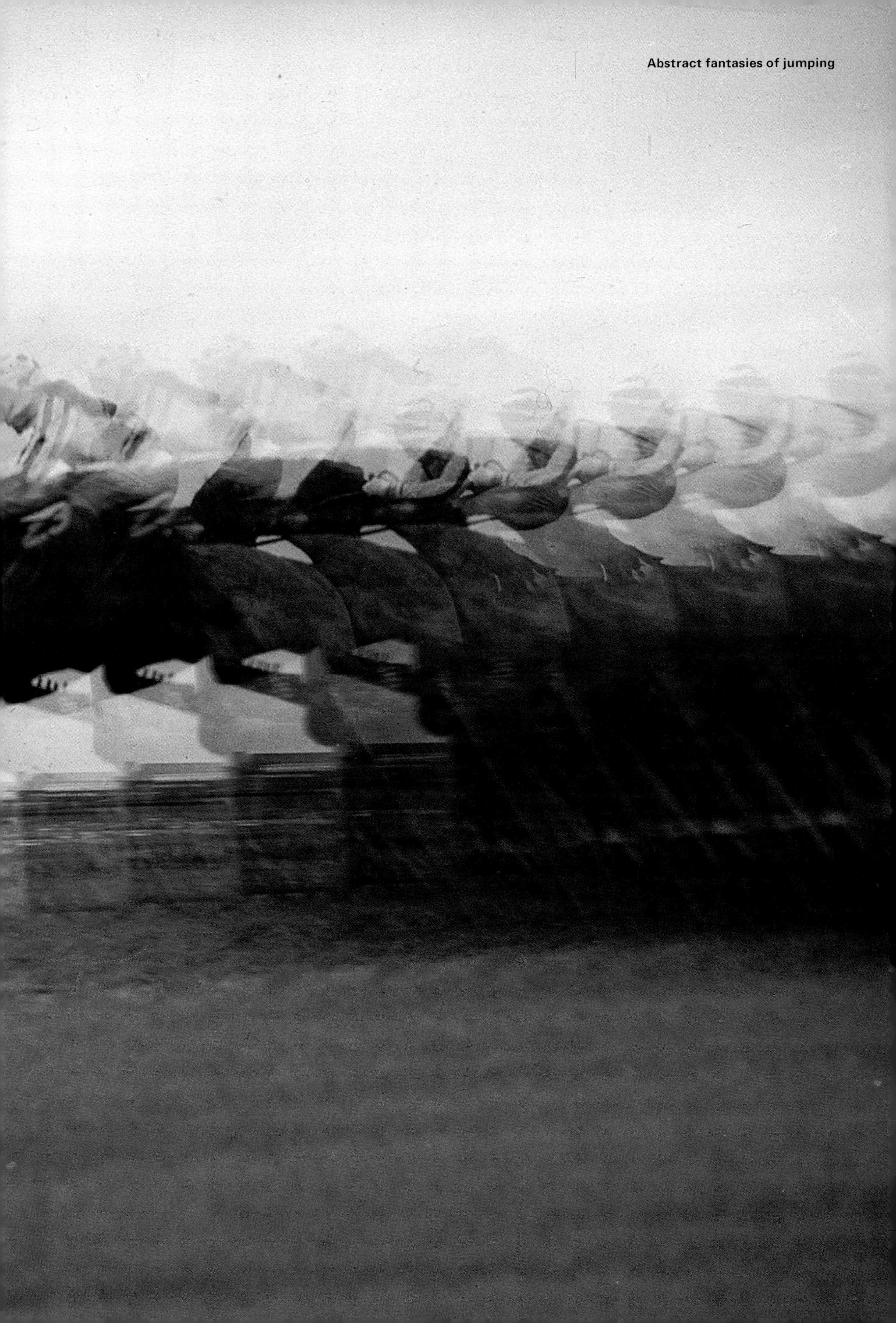

Abstract fantasies of jumping

CHELTENHAM GOLD CUP

Held at Cheltenham — a steeplechase run over $3\frac{1}{4}$ miles*   (All horses now carry 12 st)

WINNERS

Year	Winner	Age	Jockey	Starting Price
1924	Red Splash	5	F. Rees	5–1
1925	Ballinode	8	T. Leader	3–1
1926	Koko	8	J. Hamey	10–1
1927	Thrown In	11	H. Grosvenor	10–1
1928	Patron Saint	5	F. Rees	7–2
1929	Easter Hero	9	F. Rees	7–4
1930	Easter Hero	10	T. Cullinan	8–11
1931	No Race			
1932	Golden Miller	5	T. Leader	13–2
1933	Golden Miller	6	W. Stott	4–7
1934	Golden Miller	7	G. Wilson	6–5
1935	Golden Miller	8	G. Wilson	1–2
1936	Golden Miller	9	E. Williams	21–20
1937	No Race			
1938	Morse Code	9	D. Morgan	13–2
1939	Brendan's Cottage	9	G. Owen	8–1
1940	Roman Hackle	7	E. Williams	Evens
1941	Poet Prince	9	R. Burford	7–2
1942	Medoc II	8	H. Nicholson	9–2
1943–44	No Race			
1945	Red Rower	11	D. Jones	11–4
1946	Prince Regent	11	T. Hyde	4–7
1947	Fortina	6	Mr R. Black	8–1
1948	Cottage Rake	9	A. Brabazon	10–1
1949	Cottage Rake	10	A. Brabazon	4–6
1950	Cottage Rake	11	A. Brabazon	5–6
1951	Silver Fame	12	M. Molony	6–4
1952	Mont Tremblant	6	D. Dick	8–1
1953	Knock Hard	9	T. Molony	11–2
1954	Four Ten	8	T. Cusack	100–6
1955	Gay Donald	9	A. Grantham	33–1
1956	Limber Hill	9	J. Power	11–8
1957	Linwell	9	M. Scudamore	100–9
1958	Kerstin	8	S. Hayhurst	7–1
1959	Roddy Owen	10	H. Beasley	5–1
1960	Pas Seul	7	W. Rees	6–1
1961	Saffron Tartan	10	F. Winter	2–1
1962	Mandarin	11	F. Winter	7–2
1963	Mill House	6	W. Robinson	7–2
1964	Arkle	7	P. Taaffe	7–4
1965	Arkle	8	P. Taaffe	30–100
1966	Arkle	9	P. Taaffe	1–10
1967	Woodland Venture	7	T. W. Biddlecombe	100–8
1968	Fort Leney	10	P. Taaffe	11–2
1969	What a Myth	12	P. Kelleway	8–1
1970	L'Escargot	7	T. Carberry	33–1
1971	L'Escargot	8	T. Carberry	7–2
1972	Glencaraig Lady	8	F. Berry	6–1
1973	The Dikler	10	R. Barry	9–1
1974	Captain Christy	7	H. Beasley	7–1
1975	Ten Up	8	T. Carberry	2–1
1976	Royal Frolic	7	J. Burke	14–1
1977	Davy Lad	7	D. T. Hughes	14–1
1978	Midnight Court	7	J. Francome	5–2

*Distance: 1924–28, about $3\frac{1}{4}$ miles; 1929–35, 3 miles and about 3 furlongs; 1936–39, 3 miles and about 2 furlongs; 1940–45, 3 miles; 1946–57, 3 miles and about 2 furlongs; 1958, $3\frac{1}{4}$ miles; 1959–64, $3\frac{1}{4}$ miles and 130 yards; from 1965, 3 miles 2 furlongs and 76 yards.

MOST WINS

Horses

5   Golden Miller   1932–36   3   Cottage Rake   1948–50   3   Arkle   1964–66

Jockey

4   Pat Taaffe   1964–66, 1968

STATISTICS

CHAMPION HURDLE

Held at Cheltenham — a steeplechase over 2 miles 200 yards*

WINNERS

Year	Winner	Age	Jockey	Starting Price
1927	Blaris	4	G. Duller	11–10
1928	Brown Jack	6	F. Rees	4–1
1929	Royal Falcon	5	F. Rees	11–2
1930	Brown Tony	4	T. Cullinan	7–2
1931	No race			
1932	Insurance	5	T. Leader	4–5
1933	Insurance	6	W. Stott	10–11
1934	Chenango	7	D. Morgan	4–9
1935	Lion Courage	7	G. Wilson	100–8
1936	Victor Norman	5	H. Nicholson	4–1
1937	Free Fare	9	G. Pellerin	2–1
1938	Our Hope	9	Capt R. Harding	5–1
1939	African Sister	7	K. Piggott	10–1
1940	Solford	9	S. Magee	5–2
1941	Seneca	4	R. Smyth	7–1
1942	Forestation	4	R. Smyth	10–1
1943–44	No Race			
1945	Brains Trust	5	T. Rimell	9–2
1946	Distel	5	R. O'Ryan	4–5
1947	National Spirit	6	D. Morgan	7–1
1948	National Spirit	7	R. Smyth	6–4
1949	Hatton's Grace	9	A. Brabazon	100–7
1950	Hatton's Grace	10	A. Brabazon	5–2
1951	Hatton's Grace	11	T. Molony	4–1
1952	Sir Ken	5	T. Molony	3–1
1953	Sir Ken	6	T. Molony	2–5
1954	Sir Ken	7	T. Molony	4–9
1955	Clair Soleil	6	F. Winter	5–2
1956	Doorknocker	8	H. Sprague	100–9
1957	Merry Deal	7	G. Underwood	28–1
1958	Bandalore	7	G. Slack	20–1
1959	Fare Time	6	F. Winter	13–2
1960	Another Flash	6	H. Beasley	11–4
1961	Eborneezer	6	F. Winter	4–1
1962	Anzio	5	W. Robinson	11–2
1963	Winning Flair	8	Mr A. Lillingston	100–9
1964	Magic Court	6	P. McCarron	100–6
1965	Kirriemuir	5	W. Robinson	50–1
1966	Salmon Spray	8	J. Haine	4–1
1967	Saucy Kit	6	R. Edwards	100–6
1968	Persian War	5	J. Uttley	4–1
1969	Persian War	6	J. Uttley	6–4
1970	Persian War	7	J. Uttley	5–4
1971	Bula	6	P. Kelleway	15–8
1972	Bula	7	P. Kelleway	8–11
1973	Comedy of Errors	6	W. Smith	8–1
1974	Lanzarote	6	R. Pitman	7–4
1975	Comedy of Errors	8	K. White	11–8
1976	Night Nurse	5	P. Broderick	2–1
1977	Night Nurse	6	P. Broderick	15–2
1978	Monksfield	6	T. Kinane	11–2

*Distance: 1927–28, 2 miles; 1929–57, 2 miles and a few yards; 1958–60, 2 miles; 1961–64, 2 miles 100 yards; from 1965, 2 miles 200 yards.

MOST WINS

Horses

3 Hatton's Grace 1949–51   3 Sir Ken 1952–54   3 Persian War 1968–70

Jockey

4 Tim Molony 1951–54

WINNERS OF OTHER MAJOR RACES

SCHWEPPES GOLD TROPHY Run at Newbury — a handicap hurdle race over 2 miles

Year	Winner	Weight (st-lb)	Jockey	Starting Price
1963	Rosyth	10-0	J. Gifford	20–1
1964	Rosyth	10-2	J. Gifford	10–1
1965	Elan	10-7	D. Nicholson	9–2
1966	Le Vermontois	11-3	J. Gifford	15–2
1967	Hill House	10-10	J. Gifford	9–1
1968	Persian War	11-13	J. Uttley	9–2
1969	No race			
1970	No race			
1971	Cala Mesquida	10-9	J. Cook	33–1
1972	Good Review	10-9	V. O'Brien	8–1
1973	Indianapolis	10-6	J. King	15–2
1974	No race			
1975	Tammuz	10-13	W. Smith	18–1
1976	Irish Fashion	10-4	R. Barry	16–1
1977	True Lad	10-4	T. Stack	14–1
1978	No race			

WHITBREAD GOLD CUP Run at Sandown — a steeplechase over 3 miles 5 furlongs 25 yards

Year	Winner	Weight (st-lb)	Jockey	Starting Price
1957	Much Obliged	10-12	J. East	10–1
1958	Taxidermist	10-8	Mr. J. Lawrence	100–6
1959	Done Up	10-13	H. Sprague	100–6
1960	Plummers Plain	10-0	R. Hassion	20–1
1961	Pas Seul	12-0	D. Dick	8–1
1962	Frenchman's Cove	11-3	S. Mellor	7–2
1963	Hoodwinked	10-9	P. Buckley	100–7
1964	Dormant	9-7	P. Buckley	11–4
1965	Arkle	12-7	P. Taaffe	4–9
1966	What A Myth	9-8	P. Kelleway	5–4
1967	Mill House	11-11	D. Nicholson	9–2
1968	Larbawn	10-9	M. Gifford	8–1
1969	Larbawn	11-4	J. Gifford	9–2
1970	Royal Toss	10-0	R. Pitman	20–1
1971	Titus Oates	11-13	R. Barry	11–1
1972	Grey Sombrero	9-10	W. Shoemark	16–1
1973	Charlie Potheen	12-0	R. Barry	11–4
1974	The Dikler	11-13	R. Barry	5–1
1975	April Seventh	9-13	S. C. Knight	16–1
1976	Otter Way	10-10	J. King	15–2
1977	Andy Pandy	10-12	J. Burke	4–1
1978	Strombolus	10-0	T. Stack	7–1

HENNESSY COGNAC GOLD CUP Run at Newbury — a steeplechase over 3 miles 2 furlongs 82 yards

Year	Winner	Weight (st-lb)	Jockey	Starting Price
1957	Mandarin	11-0	G. Madden	8–1
1958	Taxidermist	11-1	Mr. J. Lawrence	10–1
1959	Kerstin	11-10	S. Hayhurst	4–1
1960	Knucklecracker	11-1	D. Ancil	100–7
1961	Mandarin	11-5	W. Robinson	7–1
1962	Springbok	10-8	G. Scott	15–2
1963	Mill House	12-0	W. Robinson	15–8
1964	Arkle	12-7	P. Taaffe	5–4
1965	Arkle	12-7	P. Taaffe	1–6
1966	Stalbridge Colonist	10-0	S. Mellor	25–1
1967	Rondetto	10-1	J. King	100–8
1968	Man of the West	10-0	W. Robinson	20–1
1969	Spanish Steps	11-8	J. Cook	7–1
1970	Border Mask	11-1	D. Mould	7–1
1971	Bighorn	10-11	D. Cartwright	7–1
1972	Charlie Potheen	11-4	R. Pitman	10–1
1973	Red Candle	10-4	J. Fox	12–1
1974	Royal Marshal II	10-0	G. Thorner	11–2
1975	April Seventh	11-2	A. Turnell	11–1
1976	Zeta's Son	10-9	I. Watkinson	12–1
1977	Batchelor's Hall	10-10	M. O'Halloran	11–2

A rare moment. Tommy Stack flanked by Colonel Bill Whitbread receives his trophy from HM The Queen and the Queen Mother after winning the 1978 Whitbread Gold Cup

KING GEORGE VI CHASE   Run at Kempton over 3 miles

Year	Winner	Weight (st-lb)	Jockey	Starting Price
1947	Rowland Roy	11-13	B. Marshall	5–1
1948	Cottage Rake	12-6	A. Brabazon	13–8
1949	Finnure	11-10	R. Francis	9–2
1950	Manicou	11-8	B. Marshall	5–1
1951	Statecraft	11-11	A. Grantham	100–6
1952	Halloween	11-13	F. Winter	7–4
1953	Galloway Braes	12-6	R. Morrow	9–4
1954	Halloween	11-10	F. Winter	9–2
1955	Limber Hill	11-13	J. Power	3–1
1956	Rose Park	11-7	M. Scudamore	100–6
1957	Mandarin	12-0	G. Madden	7–1
1958	Lochroe	11-7	A. Freeman	7–2
1959	Mandarin	11-5	G. Madden	5–2
1960	Saffron Tartan	11-7	F. Winter	5–2
1961	No race			
1962	No race			
1963	Mill House	12-0	W. Robinson	2–7
1964	Frenchman's Cove	11-7	S. Mellor	4–11
1965	Arkle	12-0	P. Taaffe	1–7
1966	Dormant	11-0	J. King	10–1
1967	No race			
1968	No race			
1969	Titus Oates	11-10	S. Mellor	100–30
1970	No race			
1971	The Dikler	11-7	B. Brogan	11–2
1972	Pendil	12-0	R. Pitman	4–5
1973	Pendil	12-0	R. Pitman	30–100
1974	Captain Christy	12-0	R. Coohan	5–1
1975	Captain Christy	12-0	G. Newman	11–10
1976	Royal Marshall II	11-7	G. Thorner	16–1
1977	Batchelor's Hall	11-7	M. O'Halloran	9–2

Stan Mellor the only jockey so far to have achieved the remarkable feat of riding 1000 winners over jumps!

STATISTICS

CHAMPION NATIONAL HUNT JOCKEYS AND TRAINERS

Champion NH Jockeys since 1900

Prior to 1925–26 season statistics show leading jockey for the period January to December

Year	Jockey	Wins	Year	Jockey	Wins	Year	Jockey	Wins
1900	Mr H. S. Sidney	53	1926–27	F. B. Rees	59	1952–53	F. Winter	121
1901	F. Mason	58	1927–28	W. Stott	88	1953–54	R. Francis	76
1902	F. Mason	67	1928–29	W. Stott	76	1954–55	T. Molony	67
1903	P. Woodland	54	1929–30	W. Stott	77	1955–56	F. Winter	74
1904	F. Mason	59	1930–31	W. Stott	81	1956–57	F. Winter	80
1905	F. Mason	73	1931–32	W. Stott	77	1957–58	F. Winter	82
1906	F. Mason	58	1932–33	G. Wilson	61	1958–59	T. Brookshaw	83
1907	F. Mason	59	1933–34	G. Wilson	56	1959–60	S. Mellor	68
1908	P. Cowley	65	1934–35	G. Wilson	73	1960–61	S. Mellor	118
1909	R. Gordon	45	1935–36	G. Wilson	57	1961–62	S. Mellor	80
1910	E. Piggott	67	1936–37	G. Wilson	45	1962–63	J. Gifford	70
1911	W. Payne	76	1937–38	G. Wilson	59	1963–64	J. Gifford	94
1912	I. Anthony	78	1938–39	T. F. Rimell	61	1964–65	T. Biddlecombe	114
1913	E. Piggott	60	1939–40	T. F. Rimell	24	1965–66	T. Biddlecombe	102
1914	Mr J. R. Anthony	60	1940–41	G. Wilson	22	1966–67	J. Gifford	122
1915	E. Piggott	44	1941–42	R. Smyth	12	1967–68	J. Gifford	82
1916	C. Hawkins	17	1942–43	*No racing*		1968–69	B. R. Davies	77
1917	W. Smith	15	1943–44	*No racing*			T. Biddlecombe	77
1918	G. Duller	17	1944–45	H. Nicholson	15	1969–70	B. R. Davies	91
1919	Mr H. Brown	48		T. F. Rimell	15	1970–71	G Thorner	74
1920	F. B. Rees	64	1945–46	T. F. Rimell	54	1971–72	B. R. Davies	89
1921	F. B. Rees	65	1946–47	J. Dowdeswell	58	1972–73	R. Barry	125
1922	J. Anthony	78	1947–48	B. Marshall	66	1973–74	R. Barry	94
1923	F. B. Rees	64	1948–49	T. Molony	60	1974–75	T. Stack	82
1924	F. B. Rees	108	1949–50	T. Molony	95	1975–76	J. Francome	96
1925	E. Foster	76	1950–51	T. Molony	83	1976–77	T. Stack	97
1925–26	T. Leader	61	1951–52	T. Molony	99	1977–78	J. J. O'Neill	149

Champion NH Trainers since 1946

Year	Trainer	Horses	Races won	Value (£)	Year	Trainer	Horses	Races won	Value (£)
1946–47	F. T. T. Walwyn	36	60	11,115	1962–63	K. Piggott	4	6	23,091
1947–48	F. T. T. Walwyn	40	75	16,790	1963–64	F. T. T. Walwyn	30	59	67,129
1948–49	F. T. T. Walwyn	36	64	15,563	1964–65	P. V. F. Cazalet	34	82	36,153
1949–50	P. V. F. Cazalet	29	75	18,427	1965–66	H. R. Price	29	65	42,276
1950–51	T. F. Rimell	24	60	18,381	1966–67	H. R. Price	34	73	41,222
1951–52	N. Crump	22	41	19,357	1967–68	Denys Smith	26	55	37,944
1952–53	M. V. O'Brien	4	5	15,515	1968–69	T. F. Rimell	32	62	38,344
1953–54	M. V. O'Brien	7	8	14,274	1969–70	T. F. Rimell	35	77	61,864
1954–55	H. R. Price	24	47	13,888	1970–71	F. T. Winter	29	73	60,739
1955–56	W. Hall	18	41	15,807	1971–72	F. T. Winter	37	71	62,396
1956–57	N. Crump	19	39	18,495	1972–73	F. T. Winter	37	85	79,066
1957–58	F. T. T. Walwyn	14	35	23,013	1973–74	F. T. Winter	41	89	101,782
1958–59	H. R. Price	29	52	26,550	1974–75	F. T. Winter	39	81	74,205
1959–60	P. V. F. Cazalet	25	58	22,270	1975–76	T. F. Rimell	30	49	111,740
1960–61	T. F. Rimell	28	58	34,811	1976–77	F. T. Winter	31	75	85,202
1961–62	H. R. Price	34	64	40,950	1977–78	F. T. Winter	44	90	145,915

LEADING NATIONAL HUNT JOCKEYS — NUMBER OF

	'77/78	'76/77	'75/76	'74/75	'73/74	'72/73	'71/72	'70/71	'69/70	'68/69	'67/68	'66/67	'65/66	'64/65
Stan Mellor						—	84	62	90	42	59	63	75	71
Fred Winter														—
Terry Biddlecombe				—	21	41	58	72	89	77	68	83	102	114
Bob Davies	42	50	91	63	59	69	69	89	56	91	77	40	19	1
Tim Molony														
Jeff King	36	40	52	43	40	42	66	45	37	35	33	27	41	40
Ron Barry	32	26	47	63	94	125	66	65	44	35	18	14	15	5
Josh Gifford								—	46	43	82	122	50	32
David Nicholson				—	15	29	21	21	71	33	36	63	53	58
David Mould			—	20	40	30	28	21	45	45	55	73	62	25
Tommy Stack	23	97	82	82	76	71	53	50	29	11	16	11	5	—
Graham Thorner	56	66	55	70	49	46	75	74	44	23	24	3	—	
Tim Brookshaw														—
Bob Edwards							—	55	48	35	59	64	36	46
Michael Scudamore								—	8	43	43	31	13	
Bill Rees						—	5	9	10	9	12	1	15	53
Paddy Broderick	3	14	28	23	9	24	39	38	36	27	14	50	34	48
Bryan Marshall														
Richard Pitman			—	45	79	84	59	48	34	33	23	12	7	3
Johnny Francome	83	88	96	70	30	21	19	4	—					
JonJo O'Neill	149	65	64	27	51	38	—							
Andy Turnell	29	28	35	35	44	45	41	17	20	23	23	19	8	17
Paul Kelleway	—	4	13	21	37	26	35	46	40	30	28	15	24	11
Michael Dickinson	52	53	53	29	47	44	33	28	23	11	5	—		

*Incomplete totals as these riders had winners prior to the 1947/48 season, e.g. Molony's career total was 866

WINS EACH SEASON OVER PAST 30 YEARS

'63/64	'62/63	'61/62	'60/61	'59/60	'58/59	'57/58	'56/57	'55/56	'54/55	'53/54	'52/53	'51/52	'50/51	'49/50	'48/49	'47/48	TOTAL
46	64	80	118	68	34	26	19	18	5	11	—						1035
43	29	62	82	67	74	82	80	74	65	—	121	85	38	18	1	2	923
56	41	39	18	18	8	4	—										909
—																	747
					—	35	48	70	67	45	66	99	83	95	60	34	702*
38	16	14	13	4	—												662
—																	649
94	70	61	31	12	—												643
34	37	35	37	36	25	7	6	5	1	—							643
64	23	26	32	13	4	—											606
																	606
																	585
34	36	37	90	31	83	59	21	15	25	25	19	24	29	12	9	1	550
55	50	17	19	18	11	11	1	—	1	—							519
17	33	35	45	23	58	39	21	28	34	9	11	5	—				496
38	33	59	52	44	30	51	48	6	4	6	1	—					486
35	24	13	—														459
	—	2	2	—	—		8	23	28	43	43	64	58	42	53	66	432*
—																	427
																	411
																	394
—																	384
20	14	3	12	1	2	—											382
																	378

The riders' board for the 1966 Grand National serves to remind us of some great jockeys, but also that time clouds the memory!

G⁰ NATIONAL

1	J. KING
2	P. McCARRON
3	P. KELLEWAY
4	P. TAAFFE
5	H. BEASLEY
6	G. SCOTT
7	T. W. BIDDLECOMBE
8	S. MELLOR
9	P. BUCKLEY
10	D. MOULD
12	T. CARBERRY
13	M. SCUDAMORE
14	Mr. J. LAWRENCE
15	F. SHORTT
17	OWNER
18	G. W. ROBINSON
19	T. M. JONES
21	J. LEHANE
22	T. NORMAN
23	OWNER
24	P. COWLEY

26	P. JONES
27	OWNER
28	Mc D. CROSSLEY-COOKE
29	L. McLOUGHLIN
30	G. CRAMP
31	E. PRENDERGAST
32	P. BRODERICK
33	T. HYDE
34	J. CULLEN
35	J. MORRISEY
36	Mr. N. GASALEE
37	R. COONAN
38	OWNER
39	J. MAGEE
40	J. GIFFORD
41	O. McNALLY
42	OWNER
43	J. GAMBLE
44	R. LANGLEY
45	F. CARROLL

SPEID SOOTE

Mr. T. DURANT

COURT

The most prized trophies displayed at the Cheltenham Festival Meeting

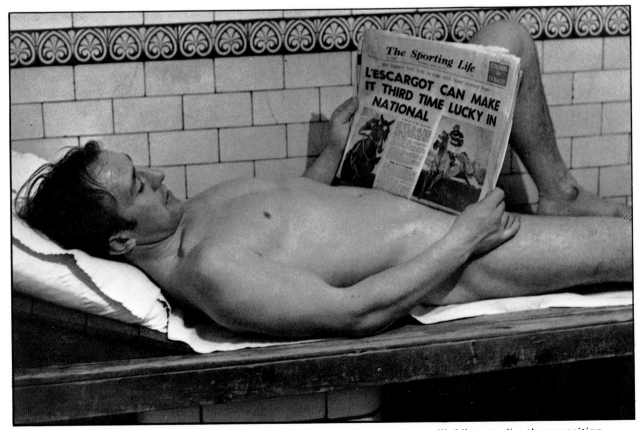

The morning of the Grand National in 1975 — the author Richard Pitman, when still riding, studies the opposition

SOME USEFUL ADDRESSES IN NATIONAL HUNT RACING

The Jockey Club
42 Portman Square
London W.1
01-486 4921

Jockeys' Association
16 The Broadway
Newbury
Berkshire
Newbury 4102

Lady Jockeys' Association
272 Malton Road
York
York 21619

Racing Information Bureau
42 Portman Square, London W.1
01-486 4571

Racehorse Owners' Association
42 Portman Square, London W.1
01-486 6977

Weatherby & Sons
42 Portman Square, London W.1
01-486 4921

Racecourse Technical Services
88 Bushey Road, Raynes Park
London S.W.20
01-947 3333

Betting Office Licensees Association
195–199 Great Portland Street
London W.1
01-637 0292

Horserace Betting Levy Board
17–23 Southampton Row
London W.C.1
01-405 5346

Bookmakers Protection Association
Sabian House
26–27 Cowcross Street
London E.C.1
01-230 0044

Index

Page numbers in italics denote illustrations

INDEX